A companion booklet to "Functional Programming in Scala"

Chapter notes, errata, hints, and answers to exercises

Rúnar Óli Bjarnason

A companion booklet to "Functional Programming in Scala"

Chapter notes, errata, hints, and answers to exercises

Rúnar Óli Bjarnason

This book is for sale at http://leanpub.com/fpinscalacompanion

This version was published on 2015-03-05

ISBN 978-1508537564

Published by Runar LLC,
Boston, Massachusetts

Contents

About this booklet

This booklet contains chapter notes, hints, answers to exercises, addenda, and errata for the book *Functional Programming in Scala*[1] by Paul Chiusano and Rúnar Bjarnason. There is no original material here, except for this brief introduction. This booklet is just a collection of material that is freely available online[2].

Why make this?

Functional Programming in Scala is a book that relies heavily on exercises. This can make it difficult to consume by *reading* rather than doing. Since the exercise answers, hints, and chapter notes are all online, a number of people have expressed difficulty studying the book on a train, on flights, in a classroom setting, or generally where there is no internet connection or where it's inconvenient to use a laptop. So what I've done is literally print all of that material in a single document, as a companion for the book itself. Its purpose is to be convenient to use as a hardcopy, with an eBook reader, a tablet, or a phone.

License

This booklet, like the material it aggregates, is released under a permissive MIT license[3]. A copy of the license is provided at the front of this booklet. You are free to make copies of this booklet and distribute them as widely as you want.

---

[1] http://manning.com/bjarnason
[2] http://github.com/fpinscala/fpinscala
[3] http://en.wikipedia.org/wiki/MIT_License

Errata

This is a list of post-publication errata for the first published version of *Functional Programming in Scala*. To submit new errata please open an issue[4] in the book's GitHub repository.

Pg xviii in About this Book: URL is incorrectly listed as https://github.com/fpinscala/fpinscla (note missing 'a'), should be https://github.com/fpinscala/fpinscala

Pg 7: In `throw new Exception`, `Exception` should not be bolded, in the code listing at the top of the page.

Pg 10: URL in footnote is incorrectly listed as https://github.com/pchiusano/fpinscala, should be https://github.com/fpinscala/fpinscala

Pg 19: Parenthetical phrase in footnote is missing a closing parenthesis.

Pg 55: `employeesByName.get("Joe")` should be `lookupByName("Joe")` at the top of the page.

Pg 82: `Int.MaxValue` is incorrectly capitalized as `Int.maxValue` in the exercise prompt for 6.1

Pg 86: Definition of `nonNegativeLessThan` at bottom of page incorrectly reuses `rng` variable for recursive call. Definition should be:

```
def nonNegativeLessThan(n: Int): Rand[Int] = { rng =>
  val (i, rng2) = nonNegativeInt(rng)
  val mod = i % n
  if (i + (n-1) - mod >= 0)
    (mod, rng2)
  else nonNegativeLessThan(n)(rng2)
}
```

Pg 74: Figure contains a typo, "strean elements" instead of "stream elements"

Pg 150: Listing 9.1 has a gratuitous nonstrict function argument in the definition of | in `ParserOps`. The definition should be:

```
case class ParserOps[A](p: Parser[A]) {
  def |[B>:A](p2: Parser[B]): Parser[B] = self.or(p,p2)
  def or[B>:A](p2: Parser[B]): Parser[B] = self.or(p,p2)
}
```

Pg 150: Examples given for `listOfN` are incorrect. Should be:

---

[4]https://github.com/fpinscala/fpinscala/issues

```
run(listOfN(3, "ab" | "cad"))("ababcad") == Right(List("ab","ab","cad"))
run(listOfN(3, "ab" | "cad"))("cadabab") == Right(List("cad","ab","ab"))
run(listOfN(3, "ab" | "cad"))("ababab") == Right(List("ab","ab","ab"))
```

Pg 184: Exercise 10.13 incorrectly defines Leaf as a case object. It should be case class:

```
case class Leaf[A](value: A) extends Tree[A]
```

Pg 187: Definition of signature for map on Option has incorrect return type, should be:

```
def map[A,B](oa: Option[A])(f: A => B): Option[B]
```

Pg 238: Definition of printLine has a typo, an extra Return constructor, should be:

```
def printLine(s: String): IO[Unit] = Suspend(() => println(s))
```

Pg 240: REPL session has a typo, should be:

```
val g = List.fill(100000)(f).foldLeft(f) {
  (a, b) => x => Suspend(() => ()).flatMap { _ => a(x).flatMap(b)}
}
```

Note: we could write a little helper function to make this nicer:

```
def suspend[A](a: => IO[A]) = Suspend(() => ()).flatMap { _ => a }

val g = List.fill(100000)(f).foldLeft(f) {
  (a, b) => x => suspend { a(x).flatMap(b) }
}
```

Pg 241: TrailRec should be TailRec at the top of the page.

Pg 285: Code snippet has an incorrectly named type parameter, currently reads:

```
case class Await[A,O](
req: Is[I]#f[A], recv: Either[Throwable,A] => Process[Is[I]#f,O]
) extends Process[Is[I]#f,R] // `R` should be `O`
```

Should read:

```
case class Await[A,O](
req: Is[I]#f[A], recv: Either[Throwable,A] => Process[Is[I]#f,O]
) extends Process[Is[I]#f,O]
```

Pg 262: List 14.3 STArray.apply has a typo, should be:

```
object STArray {
  def apply[S,A:Manifest](sz: Int, v: A): ST[S, STArray[S,A]] =
    ST(new STArray[S,A] {
      lazy val value = Array.fill(sz)(v)
    })
}
```

Pg 275: Await in the definition of loop is incorrect. Should be await.

Chapter notes

Chapter notes provide historical context, links to further reading, and additional discussion or connections to help tie the material we've covered in the book to the larger practice and research of the FP community. If you're interested, we encourage you to do some Wikipedia surfing and further exploration using some of the content covered here as a branching-off point.

Many of the chapter notes link to resources that use the Haskell language[5]. We recommend reading the *brief introduction to Haskell*, which gives an overview of Haskell for Scala programmers.

A more up-to-date version of this content is available on the FPiS community Wiki.[6]

Getting answers to your questions

If you have any questions about the book, or about functional programming in Scala (or in general), here are some suggestions:

- Ask on the scala-functional mailing list[7]
- Talk to Paul[8] and Rúnar[9] directly on Twitter.
- For questions regarding functional programming with the Scalaz library, ask on the Scalaz mailing list[10].
- Post your question on the FPiS community Wiki.[11]

Notes on chapter 1: What is functional programming?

See the Wikipedia articles on functional programming[12] and referential transparency[13].

Why functional programming matters

In this chapter we highlight some of the benefits of functional programming. A classic article that gives some justification for FP is John Hughes's *Why Functional Programming Matters*[14].

---

[5]http://www.haskell.org

[6]https://github.com/fpinscala/fpinscala/wiki

[7]https://groups.google.com/forum/#!forum/scala-functional

[8]http://twitter.com/pchiusano

[9]http://twitter.com/runarorama

[10]https://groups.google.com/forum/#!forum/scalaz

[11]https://github.com/fpinscala/fpinscala/wiki

[12]http://en.wikipedia.org/wiki/Functional_programming

[13]http://en.wikipedia.org/wiki/Referential_transparency_%28computer_science%29

[14]http://www.cs.kent.ac.uk/people/staff/dat/miranda/whyfp90.pdf

Referential transparency and side effects

We introduce functional programming as programming with *referentially transparent* expressions. Our definition of referential transparency in the chapter is a little bit simplistic, but it serves our purposes for the time being. We discuss a more expanded notion of referential transparency in chapter 14 on "local effects".

A subtlety in the definition of RT given in the chapter is the meaning of "without affecting the meaning". What is the *meaning* of a program? To answer this, we need to consider the program *with regard to* some evaluator, or in the context of some other program. That is, the meaning of a program depends very much on how we interpret or evaluate it, and whether some effect of evaluation is to be considered a *side* effect depends on the observer. For example, the fact that memory allocations occur as a side effect of data construction is not something we usually care to track or are even able to observe on the JVM. So ultimately what we consider to break referential transparency depends very much on what we can or care to observe.

See for example *What purity is and isn't*[15] for a discussion of purity with regard to an evaluator, and *Is network I/O always worth tracking?*[16] for a more philosophical take on what constitutes a side effect.

Notes on chapter 2: Getting started

We assume in this chapter that you have the Scala compiler and interpreter already up and running. See the documentation page of Scala's website[17] for more details about how to get Scala set up and links to lots of supplementary material about Scala itself.

Factorial and Fibonacci

We also assume some familiarity with the factorial function[18] and we give only a brief explanation of the Fibonacci sequence[19].

Lambda calculus

The notions of first-class and higher-order functions are formalized by the lambda calculus[20].

Parametric polymorphism

For more on parametric polymorphism, see the Wikipedia article.[21]

---

[15]http://blog.higher-order.com/blog/2012/09/13/what-purity-is-and-isnt/

[16]http://pchiusano.github.io/2014-05-21/what-effects-are-worth-tracking.html

[17]http://www.scala-lang.org/documentation/

[18]http://en.wikipedia.org/wiki/Factorial

[19]http://en.wikipedia.org/wiki/Fibonacci_number

[20]http://en.wikipedia.org/wiki/Lambda_calculus

[21]http://en.wikipedia.org/wiki/Type_variable

Parametricity

When we can "follow the type" of a function to derive the only possible implementation, we say that the definition is *given by parametricity*. See the Wikipedia article on parametricity[22], and Philip Wadler's paper *Theorems for free!*[23]

Curry

The idea of Currying[24] is named after the mathematician Haskell Curry.[25] He also discovered one of the most important results in computer science, the Curry-Howard isomorphism[26] which says that *a program is a logical proof, and the hypothesis that it proves is its type.*

Function composition

Function composition in functional programming is closely related to function composition in mathematics.[27]

FAQ for chapter 2

Are tail calls optimized if the `@annotation.tailrec` annotation isn't there?

They are still optimized, but the compiler won't warn you if it can't do the tail call optimization.

Is there a list of other annotation types somewhere?

See the Scaladoc for the Annotation class[28], and expand the 'known subclasses section'.

Is the common style to define loops using local function, rather than a (private) standalone function?

Yes, this is much more common. There's no need to pollute the namespace with helper functions you aren't expecting to be called by anyone.

Is `a || go(x)` considered a tail call? What about `a && go(x)`?

Yes

---

[22]http://en.wikipedia.org/wiki/Parametricity
[23]http://homepages.inf.ed.ac.uk/wadler/topics/parametricity.html
[24]http://en.wikipedia.org/wiki/Currying
[25]http://en.wikipedia.org/wiki/Haskell_Curry
[26]http://en.wikipedia.org/wiki/Curry%E2%80%93Howard_correspondence
[27]http://en.wikipedia.org/wiki/Function_composition
[28]http://www.scala-lang.org/api/current/index.html#scala.annotation.Annotation

Notes on chapter 3: Functional data structures

The Wikipedia article on algebraic data types[29] has further discussion about the theory behind ADTs.

Linked lists

The singly-linked list[30] (also called a *cons list*) we cover in this chapter is one of the simplest purely functional data structures. It has good performance for linear traversal, but it's not very good for random access or list concatenation.

Random access vectors and finger trees

A better structure for random access is Vector[31] in the standard library. It provides constant time (or nearly enough to constant time) access to arbitrary elements in the structure. Vectors can be seen as a specialization of the idea of a Finger Tree[32].

Difference lists

The Difference List[33] can provide efficient (constant time) concatenation of lists. The idea is that instead of having a list, we simply compose functions that operate on lists. We can compose functions in constant time, and pass an actual list to the composite function as late as possible.

Cost amortization

Reasoning about complexity of algorithms works a bit differently in a persistent (immutable) setting. We often make use of the fact that the cost of an expensive operation can be amortized over a vastly larger number of very inexpensive operations. An example of this kind of amortization is the cost of the concatenation operation on difference lists (see above). Operating on an actual list takes O(n) time, but we can spread this cost over a number of operations that we compose using the DList. This is an example of cost amortization[34].

Purely Functional Data Structures

Chris Okasaki's book *Purely Functional Data Structures*[35] (Cambridge University Press, 1999; ISBN: 0521663504) gives a thorough treatment of amortization. It is also the canonical text on efficient

---

[29]http://en.wikipedia.org/wiki/Algebraic_data_type

[30]http://en.wikipedia.org/wiki/Linked_list

[31]http://www.scala-lang.org/api/current/index.html#scala.collection.immutable.Vector

[32]http://en.wikipedia.org/wiki/Finger_tree

[33]http://www.haskell.org/haskellwiki/Difference_list

[34]http://en.wikipedia.org/wiki/Amortized_analysis

[35]http://books.google.com/books/about/Purely_Functional_Data_Structures.html?id=SxPzSTcTalAC

data structures, both classic and new, from the perspective of functional programming. We highly recommend picking up this book if you're interested in data structures. The dissertation that the book is based on is also available from Carnegie Mellon University's website[36].

Rose trees

The tree structure that we introduce at the end of the chapter is called a Rose Tree[37]. It is a nonempty multi-way tree that contains data at the nodes rather than at the leaves.

The algebra of data types

The "algebraic" in algebraic data types means something specific. This is a reference to the fact that such data types are composed of sums and products of other types. More specifically, data types form a seminearring[38].

See the following links:

- *The Algebra of Algebraic Data Types*[39] by Chris Taylor.
- *Species and Functors and Types, Oh My!*[40] by Brent Yorgey
- *Clowns to the left of me, jokers to the right*[41] by Conor McBride

Zippers

Since an algebraic data type is a type-level function involving sums and products, we can take the derivative of such a function, yielding a data structure called a zipper[42]. The zipper for a given structure is like the original structure, but with a movable "focus" or pointer into the structure. This can be used to insert, remove, and modify elements under the focus.

For example, a list zipper[43] consists of one element under focus together with two lists: one enumerating all the elements to the left of the focus, and another enumerating all the elements to the right of the focus. The focus can me moved left or right (like a zipper on a piece of clothing) and elements will move through the focus. The element under focus can then be removed or modified, and we can insert a new element by consing onto the lists to its left or right.

---

[36]http://www.cs.cmu.edu/~rwh/theses/okasaki.pdf

[37]http://en.wikipedia.org/wiki/Rose_tree

[38]http://en.wikipedia.org/wiki/Near-semiring

[39]http://chris-taylor.github.io/blog/2013/02/10/the-algebra-of-algebraic-data-types/

[40]http://www.cis.upenn.edu/~byorgey/papers/species-pearl.pdf

[41]http://personal.cis.strath.ac.uk/~conor/Dissect.pdf

[42]http://en.wikipedia.org/wiki/Zipper_%28data_structure%29

[43]http://eed3si9n.com/learning-scalaz/Zipper.html

Type inference

Scala's type system is complicated by the presence of path-dependent types and subtyping. As a result Scala has only very limited, *local* type inference.

Whereas other programming languages like Haskell or ML may have some species of Hindley-Milner[44] type inference, Scala has what's called "flow-based" inference. That is, type information "flows" from arguments to results. Given the types of the arguments, Scala is able to infer the result type of a function, unless that function is recursive. This also goes for values that are not functions, which can be considered 0-argument functions for the purpose of this discussion.

We gain type inference benefits from grouping arguments into two argument lists, as in `xs.foldRight(0)(_ + _)`. Type information flows from the first argument list to the second when inferring type arguments to a function call. Note that no inference benefit can be gained from adding more than two argument lists to a function. When inferring the type arguments to a function call, Scala's typer does not consult any argument lists beyond the first.

See the *Scala Language Specification*[45] for more information on Scala's type inference. Specifically sections 4.6.4 (Method Return Type Inference), 6.26.4 (Local Type Inference), and 8.3 (Type Parameter Inference In Patterns).

Links

- *Object-Oriented Programming Versus Abstract Data Types*[46]

FAQ for chapter 3

Why do you declare `Nil` as a `case object` instead of a `case class` within the definition of our functional `sealed trait List`?

`case object` is more appropriate because `Nil` is a singleton. We can still use pattern matching in this case. However, there won't be a companion object with `apply`, `unapply`, etc. `case class Nil` will actually cause an error because case classes require an explicit parameter list:

```
scala> case class Nil
<console>:1: error: case classes without a parameter list are not allowed;
use either case objects or case classes with an explicit `()' as a parameter list.
case class Nil
            ^
```

---

[44]http://en.wikipedia.org/wiki/Hindley%E2%80%93Milner_type_system
[45]http://www.scala-lang.org/docu/files/ScalaReference.pdf
[46]http://www.cs.utexas.edu/users/wcook/papers/OOPvsADT/CookOOPvsADT90.pdf

Notes on chapter 4: Handling errors without exceptions

Partial and total functions

A partial function[47], as opposed to a *total function*, is a function that is not defined for some of its inputs. That is, it's not true for partial functions that every value of the input type maps to a value of the output type. There are different approaches to representing this kind of function, but in functional programming we commit to using only total functions. The approach we take in this chapter is to augment the return type of partial functions to make it "the same size" as the input type.

For example, the `Option[T]` type simply adds one data constructor, `None`, to the underlying type `T`. That way we can have a total function of type `X => Option[T]` represent a partial function from `X` to `T`. Wherever the function is not defined for a given `X`, we simply map that value to `None` in the result type.

Turing completeness and the halting problem

Another possibility in languages that are Turing complete[48], which includes Scala, is that a function may "hang" or "run forever" in an infinite loop. Functions that do this are also considered to be partial. However, in a language like Scala we cannot prevent this kind of partiality nor can we recover from it in the general case. It is equivalent to the halting problem[49].

Bottoms

A program that hangs (by running in an infinite loop) or crashes (by throwing an exception) is said to "evaluate to bottom". The term "bottom" (sometimes "falsum") comes from logic, where it is used to denote a contradiction. The Curry-Howard isomorphism[50] says that types are propositions, and a program of a given type is a proof of that proposition. Since a non-terminating program can have *any type*, we can say that it's a proof of *every proposition*. This is exactly like the situation with contradictions in logic–if you assume a contradiction, you can prove any proposition.

Total languages

Some programming languages are total languages[51], and do not provide facilities for unbounded recursion like Scala does. A program in such a language *provably terminates*, and there are no

---

[47]http://en.wikipedia.org/wiki/Partial_function

[48]http://en.wikipedia.org/wiki/Turing-complete

[49]http://en.wikipedia.org/wiki/Halting_problem

[50]http://en.wikipedia.org/wiki/Curry%E2%80%93Howard_correspondence

[51]http://en.wikipedia.org/wiki/Total_functional_programming

bottoms. The price of this is that such languages are not Turing complete, since there exist in theory some programs that they cannot express, although the capabilities of total languages like Agda[52], Coq[53], and Idris[54] are suggesting to us that Turing completeness may not be necessary for a large majority of useful programs. Also see the paper Total Functional Programming[55].

Covariance and contravariance

In this chapter we briefly touch on the subject of *variance* in Scala. This is a feature of the subtyping in Scala's type system. Throughout this book we tend to largely ignore this feature since we find that in practice it unnecessarily complicates Scala's type system. We find that it's not beneficial to functional programming and can in fact often be a barrier to good API design. Outside of the language specification[56], there is not much freely available documentation of how variance works in Scala specifically, but for a general discussion see the Wikipedia article on covariance and contravariance.[57]

Variance in `Option[+A]`

Recall that the `+A` in `Option[+A]` declares that, for example, `Option[Dog]` is a subtype of `Option[Animal]` (and that `None`, having type `Option[Nothing]`, is a subtype of any `Option[A]`). But why are we forced to accept a *supertype* of `A` (as indicated by the `[B >: A]`) in `getOrElse` and `orElse`?

Another way to state the `+A` annotation is that we're telling Scala that in *all contexts* it's safe to convert this `A` to a supertype of A—Dog may be converted to `Animal`, for instance. Scala (correctly) won't let us provide this annotation unless all members of a type *agree* it's safe to do this conversion. Let's see the contradiction if `orElse` had the following (simpler) signature:

```scala
trait Option[+A] {
  def orElse(o: Option[A]): Option[A]

  . . .

}
```

This is problematic—since `orElse` is a function accepting an `Option[A]` as an argument, this is a place where we may only convert `A` to a *subtype* of `A`. Why? Like any function, `orElse` must be passed a subtype of the type of argument it accepts—a `Dog => R` can be called with a `Poodle` or `Dog`, not an arbitrary `Animal`. (We therefore say that such functions are *contravariant* in their argument type.) But the fact that we have a member of `Option[A]` that only allows subtypes of `A` contradicts the `+A` in `Option[A]`, which says that in *all contexts* we can convert this `A` to any *supertype* of `A`. Contradictions

[52]http://en.wikipedia.org/wiki/Agda_(programming_language)

[53]http://coq.inria.fr/

[54]http://www.idris-lang.org/

[55]http://www.jucs.org/jucs_10_7/total_functional_programming/jucs_10_07_0751_0768_turner.pdf

[56]http://www.scala-lang.org/docu/files/ScalaReference.pdf

[57]http://en.wikipedia.org/wiki/Covariance_and_contravariance_%28computer_science%29

like this will result in a compile error like `"covariant type A occurs in contravariant position"`. Scala must enforce that no such contradictions exist, or we could circumvent the type-checker and easily write programs that gave a type error at runtime, in the form of a `ClassCastException`.

The more complicated signature fixes the contradiction by not mentioning `A` in any of the function arguments:

```
def orElse[B >: A](o: Option[B]): Option[B]
```

Covariant and contravariant positions

A type is in *covariant position* (positive) if it is in the result type of a function, or more generally is the type of a value that is *produced*.

A type is in *contravariant position* (negative) if it's in the argument type of a function, or more generally is the type of a value that is *consumed*.

For example, in `def foo(a: A): B`, the type `A` is in contravariant position and `B` is in covariant position, all things being equal.

We can extend this reasoning to higher-order functions. In `def foo(f: A => B): C`, the type `A => B` appears in negative (contravariant) position. This means the variance of the types `A` and `B` is flipped. The type `A` appears in a negative position of a type in negative position. So just like the negation of a negative is a positive, this means `A` is actually in covariant position. And since `B` is in the covariant position of a type in contravariant position, it's the negation of a positive, so `B` is in contravariant position overall.

We can always count the position of a polymorphic type this way. Result types are positive, and argument types are negative. The arguments to arguments are positive, arguments to arguments to arguments are negative, and so on.

Notes on chapter 5: Strictness and laziness

Non-strictness vs laziness

The Haskell website[58] has a good explanation of the difference between *non-strictness* and *laziness*.

In short, "non-strict" just means "not strict". There are many possible evaluation strategies[59] one could employ when evaluating a program, and strict evaluation[60] is one of them. Non-strict evaluation[61] is a *class* of evaluation strategies, and lazy evaluation[62] is one non-strict strategy (also known as "call-by-need").

---

[58]http://www.haskell.org/haskellwiki/Lazy_vs._non-strict

[59]http://en.wikipedia.org/wiki/Evaluation_strategy

[60]http://en.wikipedia.org/wiki/Strict_evaluation

[61]http://en.wikipedia.org/wiki/Non-strict_evaluation#Non-strict_evaluation

[62]http://en.wikipedia.org/wiki/Lazy_evaluation

In Scala, non-strict arguments are sometimes called "by name" arguments, in reference to the fact that the evaluation strategy Scala employs for those arguments is call-by-name[63]. We can turn an argument into call-by-need by caching it in a `lazy val` inside the function:

```scala
def pairIf[A](b: Boolean, x: => A) = {
  lazy val y = x
  if (b) Some((y, y)) else None
}
```

This function will evaluate x only once, or never if the boolean b is `false`. If we said (x, x) instead of (y, y), it would evaluate x twice.

The chapter explains that when an expression does not terminate, it is said to evaluate to *bottom*. At first glance this is counter intuitive because there is a natural tendency to think of infinity as having *no* bottom. But the bottom to which the chapter refers is actually the bottom type[64]. See Haskell's definition of bottom[65] for a more thorough description. Scala refers to it as Nothing[66], which is at the *bottom* of the inheritance hierarchy.

Corecursion and codata

The Wikipedia article on corecursion[67] is a good starting point for understanding the concept.

The article on Coinduction[68] has some further links. Dan Piponi's article *Data and Codata*[69] talks about corecursion as "guarded" recursion.

Ralf Hinze's paper *Reasoning about Codata*[70] brings equational reasoning to corecursive programs by employing applicative functors. Hinze's paper will be more comprehensible to readers who have finished part 3 of our book.

Tying the knot

Non-strictness allows us to create cyclic streams such as:

```scala
val cyclic: Stream[Int] = 0 #:: 1 #:: cyclic
```

---

[63] http://en.wikipedia.org/wiki/Call_by_name#Call_by_name

[64] http://en.wikipedia.org/wiki/Bottom_type

[65] http://www.haskell.org/haskellwiki/Bottom

[66] http://www.scala-lang.org/api/current/#scala.runtime.Nothing\protect\char"0024\relax

[67] http://en.wikipedia.org/wiki/Corecursion

[68] http://en.wikipedia.org/wiki/Coinduction

[69] http://blog.sigfpe.com/2007/07/data-and-codata.html

[70] http://www.cs.ox.ac.uk/ralf.hinze/publications/CEFP09.pdf

This may seem like it shouldn't work. The stream is referencing itself in its own tail! But the trick is that the `#::` constructor is non-strict in its second argument. The evaluation of `cyclic` will stop without expanding the expression `1 #:: cyclic`. It's not until somebody takes the `tail` of the `tail` of `cyclic` that the recursive reference is expanded, and again it expands only one element at a time, allowing for an infinite, cyclic stream.

Note that the `cyclic` stream is reusing its own structure. `cyclic.tail.tail` is not a new stream that looks like `cyclic`. It really is the same object as `cyclic` in every sense:

```scala
scala> cyclic.tail.tail eq cyclic
res0: Boolean = true
```

This technique is sometimes called "Tying the Knot". For more information see the Haskell.org article[71].

However, be careful of creating such structures using the Scala standard library's `Stream`. They can be quite fragile. The reason is that `scala.Stream` is is strict in the head element and it will also memoize[72] the computed contents, which can lead to memory leaks.

Stream.apply

Be careful using Stream.apply, both in the standard library and in the exercises: they are constructed using *repeated parameters*, which are always strict. This means that e.g.

```scala
Stream({println("One"); 1}, {println("Two"); 2}, {println("Three"); 3})
```

will immediately print One, Two, Three. Although the Stream will be constructed lazily, the contents have already been evaluated.

For truly lazily constructed Streams you can always resort to `#::` (which still evaluates the head value strictly!) or nested cons(..,cons(..,..)) operators in the exercises.

Notes on chapter 6: Purely functional state

State in Scalaz

The Scalaz library[73] supplies a `State` data type[74] that is a specialization of a more general type `IndexedStateT`[75], where `State[S,A] = IndexedStateT[Id, S, S, A]` and `Id[A] = A`.

---

[71] http://www.haskell.org/haskellwiki/Tying_the_Knot

[72] http://en.wikipedia.org/wiki/Memoization

[73] http://github.com/scalaz/scalaz

[74] http://docs.typelevel.org/api/scalaz/stable/7.1.0-M3/doc/#scalaz.package\protect\char"0024\relax\protect\char"0024\relaxState\protect\char"0024\relax

[75] http://docs.typelevel.org/api/scalaz/stable/7.1.0-M3/doc/#scalaz.IndexedStateT

You do not need to understand this more general type if you just want to use State[S,A]. But the general type has two additional features:

1. The start state and end state of a state transition can have different types. That is, it's not necessarily a transition S => (S, A), but S1 => (S2, A). The ordinary State type is where S1 and S2 are fixed to be the same type.

2. It is a *monad transformer*[76] (see chapter 12). The type of a state transition is not S => (S, A), but S => F[(S, A)] for some monad[77] F (see chapter 11). The monad transformer allows us to bind across F and State in one operation. The ordinary State type is where this monad is fixed to be the identity monad Id.

Pseudorandom number generation

The Wikipedia article on pseudorandom number generators[78] is a good place to start for more information about such generators. It also makes the distinction between *random* and *pseudorandom* generation.

There's also a good page on Linear congruential generators[79], including advantages and disadvantages and links to several implementations in various languages.

Deterministic finite state automata

The State data type can be seen as a model of Mealy Machines[80] in the following way. Consider a function f of a type like A => State[S, B]. It is a transition function in a Mealy machine where

- The type S is the set of states
- State[S, B]'s representation is a function of type S => (B, S). Then the argument to that function is the initial state.
- The type A is the input alphabet of the machine.
- The type B is the output alphabet of the machine.

The function f itself is the transition function of the machine. If we expand A => State[S, B], it is really A => S => (B, S) under the hood. If we uncurry that, it becomes (A, S) => (B, S) which is identical to a transition function in a Mealy machine. Specifically, the output is determined both by the state of type S and the input value of type A.

Contrast this with a Moore machine[81], whose output is determined solely by the current state. A Moore machine could be modeled by a data type like the following:

---

[76]http://en.wikipedia.org/wiki/Monad_transformer

[77]http://en.wikipedia.org/wiki/Monad_%28functional_programming%29

[78]http://en.wikipedia.org/wiki/Pseudorandom_number_generator

[79]http://en.wikipedia.org/wiki/Linear_congruential_generator

[80]http://en.wikipedia.org/wiki/Mealy_machine

[81]http://en.wikipedia.org/wiki/Moore_machine

```
case class Moore[S, I, A](t: (S, I) => S, g: S => A)
```

Together with an initial state s of type S. Here:

- S is the set of states.
- I is the input alphabet.
- A is the output alphabet.
- t is the transition function mapping the state and an input value to the next state.
- g is the output function mapping each state to the output alphabet.

As with Mealy machines, we could model the transition function and the output function as a single function:

```
type Moore[S, I, A] = S => (I => S, A)
```

Since both the transition function t and the output function g take a value of type S, we can take that value as a single argument and from it determine the transition function of type I => S as well as the output value of type A at the same time.

Mealy and Moore machines are related in a way that is interesting to explore.

Lenses

If we specialize Moore so that the input and output types are the same, we get a pair of functions t: (S, A) => S and g: S => A. We can view these as (respectively) a "getter" and a "setter" of A values on the type S:

```
get: S => A
set: (S, A) => S
```

Imagine for example where S is Person and A is Name.

```
type Name = String
```

```
case class Person(name: Name, age: Int)
```

A function getName would have the type Person => Name, and setName would have the type (Person, Name) => Person. In the latter case, given a Person and a Name, we can set the name of the Person and get a new Person with the new name.

The getter and setter together form what's called a *lens*. A lens "focuses" on a part of a larger structure, and allows us to modify the value under focus. A simple model of lenses is:

```
case class Lens[A, B](get: A => B, set: (A, B) => A)
```

Where A is the larger structure, and B is the part of that structure that is under focus.

Importantly, lenses *compose*. That is, if you have a Lens[A,B], and a Lens[B,C], you can get a composite Lens[A,C] that focuses on a C of a B of an A.

Lenses are handy to use with the State data type. Given a State[S,A]. If we're interested in looking at or modifying a portion of the state, and the portion has type T, it can be useful to focus on a portion of the state that we're interested in using a Lens[S,T]. The getter and setter of a lens can be readily converted to a State action:

```
def getS[S,A](l: Lens[S, A]): State[S,A] =
  State(s => (l.get(s), s))

def setS[S,A](l: Lens[S, A], a: A): State[S,Unit] =
  State(s => (l.set(s, a), ()))
```

We cannot, however, turn a State action into a Lens, for the same reason that we cannot convert a Moore machine into a Mealy machine.

See the Scalaz library's lenses[82], the Monocle library for Scala[83], and the Lens library for Haskell[84], for more information about how to take advantage of lenses.

Stack overflow issues in State

The State data type as represented in chapter 6 suffers from a problem with stack overflows for long-running state machines. The problem is that flatMap contains a function call that is in tail position, but this tail call is not eliminated on the JVM.

The solution is to use a *trampoline*. Chapter 13 gives a detailed explanation of this technique. See also Rúnar's paper *Stackless Scala With Free Monads*[85].

Using the trampolining data type TailRec from chapter 13, a stack-safe State data type could be written as follows:

```
case class State[S,A](run: S => TailRec[(A, S)])
```

This is identical to the State data type we present in chapter 6, except that the result type of run is TailRec[(S,A)] instead of just (S,A). See chapter 13 for a thorough discussion of TailRec. The important part is that the *result type* of the State transition function needs to be a data type like TailRec that gets run at a later time by a tail recursive trampoline function.

---

[82]http://eed3si9n.com/learning-scalaz/Lens.html

[83]https://github.com/julien-truffaut/Monocle

[84]https://www.fpcomplete.com/school/to-infinity-and-beyond/pick-of-the-week/a-little-lens-starter-tutorial

[85]http://blog.higher-order.com/assets/trampolines.pdf

Notes on chapter 7: Purely functional parallelism

FP has a long history of using combinator libraries for expressing parallelism, and there are a lot of variations of the general idea. The main design choices in this sort of library are around how explicit to make the *forking* and *joining* of parallel computations. That is, should the API force the programmer to be fully explicit about when parallel tasks are being forked off into a separate logical thread, or should this be done automatically? And similarly, when waiting for the results of multiple logical threads (say, for the implementation of map2), should the order of these joins be something the programmer explicitly specifies or chosen by the framework?

The library we developed in this chapter sits somewhere in the middle—it is explicit about where tasks are forked, but not when tasks are joined (notice that map2 picks the order it waits for the two tasks whose results it is combining). The join order can be made more explicit. Simon Marlow, one of the GHC Haskell[86] developers, discusses this in Parallel programming in Haskell with explicit futures[87]. Also see the full paper, Seq no more: Better Strategies for Parallel Haskell[88], which does a nice job of explaining some of the history of approaches for parallelism in Haskell.

Note that because Scala is a strict-by-default language, being more explicit about the join order isn't necessarily as beneficial as in Haskell. That is, we can get away with reasoning about join order much like we think about evaluation in normal strict function application.

This style of library isn't particularly good at expressing *pipeline parallelism* that's possible when transforming streams of data. For instance, if we have a Stream[Int] of 10000 items, and we wish to square each value, then compute a running sum of the squared values, there is a potential for parallelism—as we are squaring values, we can be passing the squared values off to another consumer that is emitting the running sum of the values it receives. We'll be discussing stream processing and pipeline parallelism more in part 4.

Notes about map fusion

We noted in this chapter that one of our laws for Par, sometimes called *map fusion*, can be used as an optimization:

```
map(map(y)(g))(f) == map(y)(f compose g)
```

That is, rather than spawning a separate parallel computation to compute the second mapping, we can fold it into the first mapping. We mentioned that our representation of Par doesn't allow for this, as it's too 'opaque'. If we make Par a proper data type and give it constructors that we can pattern match on, then it's easy to implement map fusion:

---

[86]http://www.haskell.org/ghc/

[87]http://ghcmutterings.wordpress.com/2010/08/20/parallel-programming-in-haskell-with-explicit-futures/

[88]http://www.haskell.org/~simonmar/papers/strategies.pdf

```scala
trait Par[+A] {
  def map[B](f: A => B): Par[B] = this match {
    case MapPar(p, g) => MapPar(p, g andThen f)
    case _ => MapPar(
  }
case class MapPar[A,+B](par: Par[A], f: A => B) extends Par[B]
```

Baking ad hoc optimization rules like this into our data type works, but it can sometimes get unwieldy, and it's not very modular (we don't get to reuse code if there's some other data type needing similar optimizations). There are various ways of factoring out these sorts of optimizations so our core data type (be it Par or some other type) stays clean, and the optimization is handled as a separate concern. Edward Kmett has a nice blog series discussing this approach[89]. Before embarking on that series you'll need to be familiar with the content in part 3 of this book, and you should read the Haskell appendix as well.

Notes on chapter 8: Property-based testing

The style of combinator library for testing we developed in this chapter was introduced in a 2000 paper by Koen Claessen and John Hughes, *QuickCheck: A Lightweight Tool for Random Testing of Haskell Programs*[90] (PDF). In that paper, they presented a Haskell library, called QuickCheck[91], which became quite popular in the FP world and has inspired similar libraries in other languages, including ScalaCheck[92]. Many programmers who adopt this style of testing find it to be extraordinarily effective (see, for instance, this experience report[93] on Tom Moertel's blog[94]).

The wikipedia page on QuickCheck[95] and the Haskell wiki page[96] are good places to start if you're interested in learning more about these sorts of libraries. QuickCheck sparked a number of variations, including the Haskell library SmallCheck[97], which is focused on exhaustive enumeration.

Although property-based testing works quite well for testing pure functions, it can also be used for testing imperative code. The general idea is to generate *lists of instructions*, which are then fed to an interpreter of these actions. We then check that the pre and post-conditions are as expected. Here's a simple example of testing the mutable stack implementation from Scala's standard library (API docs[98]):

---

[89]http://comonad.com/reader/2011/free-monads-for-less/

[90]http://www.eecs.northwestern.edu/~robby/courses/395-495-2009-fall/quick.pdf

[91]http://en.wikipedia.org/wiki/QuickCheck

[92]https://github.com/rickynils/scalacheck/wiki/User-Guide

[93]http://blog.moertel.com/pages/seven-lessons-from-the-icfp-programming-contest

[94]http://blog.moertel.com/

[95]http://en.wikipedia.org/wiki/QuickCheck

[96]http://www.haskell.org/haskellwiki/Introduction_to_QuickCheck

[97]https://github.com/feuerbach/smallcheck

[98]http://www.scala-lang.org/api/current/scala/collection/mutable/ArrayStack.html

```
forAll(Gen.listOf(Gen.choose(1,10))) { l =>
  val buf = new collection.mutable.ArrayStack[Int]
  val beforeSize = buf.size
  l.foreach(buf.push)
  buf.beforeSize == 0 && buf.size == l.size
}
```

In this case, the "interpreter" is the `push` method on `ArrayStack`, which modifies the stack in place, and the "instructions" are simply the integers from the input list. But the basic idea can be extended to testing richer interfaces–for instance, we could generate instructions that could either `push` or `pop` elements from an `ArrayStack` (perhaps represented as a `List[Option[Int]]`), and write a property that sequences of `push` and `pop` preserve the invariants of `ArrayStack` (for instance, the final size of the stack should be the number of `push` calls minus the number of `pop` calls). Care must be taken to craft generators that produce valid sequences of instructions (for instance, `pop` without a corresponding prior `push` is not a valid input).

Similar ideas have been used for testing thread safety of concurrent programs. (See *Finding Race Conditions in Erlang with QuickCheck and PULSE*[99] (PDF)) The key insight here is that thread-safe code does not allow the nondeterminism of thread scheduling to be *observable*. That is, for any *partial order* of instructions run concurrently, we ought to able to find some single-threaded linear sequence of these instructions with the same observable behavior (this criteria is often called *linearizability*). For instance, if our `ArrayStack` were thread-safe, we would expect that if 2 `push` operations were performed sequentially, followed by two `pop` operations and two `push` operations performed concurrently, this should yield the same result as some deterministic linear sequence of these `push` and `pop` operations). There are some subtleties and interesting questions about how to model this and how to report and minimize failing test cases. In particular, doing it the "obvious" way ends up being intractable due to having to search through a combinatorial number of interleavings to find one that satisfies the observation. The Erlang paper linked above has more details, in particular see section 4. You may be interested to explore how to incorporate these ideas into the library we developed, possibly building on the parallelism library we wrote last chapter.

Lastly, we mention that one design goal of some libraries in this style is to avoid having to *explicitly* construct generators. The QuickCheck library makes use of a Haskell type class to provide instances of `Gen` "automatically", and this idea has also been borrowed by ScalaCheck[100]. This can certainly be convenient, especially for simple examples, though we often find that explicit generators are necessary to capture all the interesting constraints on the shape or form of the inputs to a function.

---

[99]http://www.protest-project.eu/upload/paper/icfp070-claessen.pdf
[100]https://github.com/rickynils/scalacheck/wiki/User-Guide

Notes on chapter 9: Parser combinators

Different approaches to functional design

There are many different approaches to functional design. The approach we take in this chapter we are calling "algebraic design" to emphasize the fact that we are mainly concerned with the abstract data types and laws of our API. The actual representation is a later concern, and we choose a representation that best facilitates our algebra. This perspective is common to Category Theory[101], where mathematical objects (or a *type* in the more concretely programming-related case) are defined solely by their relationship to other objects, not their "internal" structure.

Conal Elliott[102] advocates for an approach he calls denotational design[103], also see this nice exposition by Luke Palmer[104]. In this style of design, the choice of a *precise meaning* or *denotation* (see denotational semantics[105]) for the data types in our library guides the design process. This denotation is not (necessarily) similar to the actual concrete representation we ultimately select when implementing our library–that happens later. The denotation is instead a hopefully simple, precise mathematical object that lets us understand what the data types of our library and their various operations *mean* (in terms of how they transform these denotations). In this style of design, we begin with some initial idea of a denotation for our data type, and refine this denotation in response to the operations we wish to support.

There is no "right" answer in approaches to the design of software, and the higher your perspective, the more the lines between different approaches blur.

Design issues in parser combinator libraries

Parser combinator libraries are very common in the FP world, and there are a lot of different variations. A few of the key design issues:

Error reporting: Generating good error messages is a delicate problem, and is easy to get wrong. The overall error-reporting strategy developed in this chapter is most similar to Parsec[106], a widely used parsing library in Haskell, though Parsec does not support the *nested* error messages we developed here. A key factor for good error reporting is having a clear model for *when backtracking is allowed to occur* and giving the programmer the ability to control this when specifying the grammar. We chose to adopt Parsec's convention that all parsers commit by default if they consume at least one character, and that the `attempt` combinator "undoes" this commit. Another choice is to *not* have parsers commit by default, and introduce a separate `commit` combinator (which is still "undone" by `attempt`). This has the same expressiveness but we find it is not usually the best default since most

---

[101]http://en.wikipedia.org/wiki/Category_theory

[102]http://conal.net/

[103]http://conal.net/papers/type-class-morphisms

[104]http://lukepalmer.wordpress.com/2008/07/18/semantic-design/

[105]http://en.wikipedia.org/wiki/Denotational_semantics

[106]http://legacy.cs.uu.nl/daan/parsec.html

grammars require little lookahead. Interestingly, the grammar ends up looking almost the same with the introduction of an explicit `commit`: the leaf-level `token` parser is usually wrapped in `commit`, and higher levels of the grammar that require more lookahead use `attempt`.

Input handling: Is the input type fixed to be `String` or can parsers be polymorphic over any sequence of tokens? The library developed in this chapter chose `String` for simplicity and speed. Separate tokenizers are not as commonly used with parser combinators—the main reason to use a separate tokenizer would be for speed, which is usually addressed by building a few fast low-level primitive like `regex` (which checks whether a regular expression matches a prefix of the input string).

Having the input type be an arbitrary `Seq[A]` results in a library that could in principle be used for other sorts of computations (for instance, we can "parse" a sum from a `Seq[Int]`). There are usually better ways of doing these other sorts of tasks (see the discussion of stream processing in part 4 of the book) and we have found that there isn't much advantage in generalizing the library we have here to other input types.

We can define a similar set of combinators for parsing *binary* formats. Binary formats rarely have to deal with lookahead, ambiguity, and backtracking, and have simpler error reporting needs, so often a more specialized binary parsing library is sufficient. Some examples of binary parsing libraries are Data.Binary[107] in Haskell, which has inspired similar libraries in other languages, for instance scodec[108] in Scala.

You may be interested to explore generalizing or adapting the library we wrote enough to handle binary parsing as well (to get good performance, you may want to try using the specialized annotation[109] to avoid the overhead of boxing and unboxing that would otherwise occur).

Streaming parsing and push vs. pull: It is possible to make a parser combinator library that can operate on huge inputs, larger than what is possible or desirable to load fully into memory. Related to this is is the ability to produce results in a streaming fashion—for instance, as the raw bytes of an HTTP request are being read, the parse result is being constructed. The two general approaches here are to allow the parser to *pull* more input from its input *source*, and inverting control and *pushing* chunks of input to our parsers (this is the approach taken by the popular Haskell library attoparsec[110]), which may report they are finished, failed, or requiring more input after each chunk. We will discuss this more in part 4 when discussing stream processing.

Handling of ambiguity and left-recursion: The parsers developed in this chapter scan input from left to right and use a left-biased `or` combinator which selects the "leftmost" parse if the grammar is ambiguous—these are called LL parsers[111]. This is a design choice. There are other ways to handle ambiguity in the grammar—in GLR parsing[112], roughly, the `or` combinator explores both branches simultaneously and the parser can return multiple results if the input is ambiguous. (See Daniel

---

[107]http://code.haskell.org/binary/

[108]https://github.com/scodec/scodec

[109]http://www.scala-notes.org/2011/04/specializing-for-primitive-types/

[110]http://hackage.haskell.org/packages/archive/attoparsec/0.10.2.0/doc/html/Data-Attoparsec-ByteString.html

[111]http://en.wikipedia.org/wiki/LL_parser

[112]http://en.wikipedia.org/wiki/GLR_parser

Spiewak's series on GLR parsing[113] also his paper[114]) GLR parsing is more complicated, there are difficulties around supporting good error messages, and we generally find that its extra capabilities are not needed in most parsing situations.

Related to this, the parser combinators developed here cannot directly handle *left-recursion*, for instance:

```
def expr = (int or double) or (
           expr ** "+" ** expr ) or (
           "(" ** expr ** ")" )
```

This will fail with a stack overflow error, since we will keep recursing into `expr`. The invariant that prevents this is that all branches of a parser must consume at least one character before recursing. In this example, we could do this by simply factoring the grammar a bit differently:

```
def leaf = int or double or ("(" ** expr ** ")")
def expr = leaf.sep("+")
```

Where `sep` is a combinator that parses a list of elements, ignoring some delimiter ("separator") that comes between each element (it can be implemented in terms of `many`). This same basic approach can be used to handle operator precedence–for instance, if `leaf` were a parser that included binary expressions involving multiplication, this would make the precedence of multiplication higher than that of addition. Of course, it is possible to write combinators to abstract out patterns like this. It is also possible to write a monolithic combinator that uses a more efficient (but specialized) algorithm[115] to build operator parsers.

Other interesting areas to explore related to parsing

- *Monoidal and incremental parsing*: This deals with the much harder problem of being able to incrementally reparse input in the presences of inserts and deletes, like what might be nice to support in a text-editor or IDE. See Edward Kmett's articles on this[116] as a starting point.
- *Purely applicative parsers*: If we stopped before adding `flatMap`, we would still have a useful library–context-sensitivity is not often required, and there are some interesting tricks that can be played here. See this stack overflow answer[117] for a discussion and links to more reading.

---

[113]http://www.codecommit.com/blog/scala/unveiling-the-mysteries-of-gll-part-1

[114]http://www.cs.uwm.edu/~dspiewak/papers/generalized-parser-combinators.pdf

[115]http://en.wikipedia.org/wiki/Shunting-yard_algorithm

[116]http://comonad.com/reader/2009/iteratees-parsec-and-monoid/

[117]http://stackoverflow.com/questions/7861903/what-are-the-benefits-of-applicative-parsing-over-monadic-parsing

Single pass parsing

Lastly, we mentioned that the JSON parser we wrote in this chapter was rather dumb in that it only constructed a parse tree. This is unfortunate–we will typically then have to traverse this parse tree to extract some meaningful type from the parse tree after the fact. We could instead build up whatever type we wish *as we go*. The general idea is to parameterize our grammar on functions that describe what to do at each level of the parse tree:

```
def array[A,B](value: Parser[A])(f: List[A] => B): Parser[B] =
  "[" *> value.sep(",").map(f) <* "]"
  // `*>` ignores the left parse result, in this case the `"["`,
  // and `<*` ignores the right parse result, in this case the `"]"`.
```

This parses a JSON array, but rather than building a JArray, immediately converts the result to B using the given function, where B might be some more meaningful type. The same strategy can be applied for the rest of the grammar.

Notes on chapter 10: Monoids

Monoids in category theory

In category theory[118], a monoid[119] is a category[120] with one object.

A *category* is a purely algebraic structure consisting of "objects" and "arrows" between them, much like a directed graph with nodes and edges between them. A category will have objects like A, B, C, etc. and arrows between objects. Importantly, arrows *compose*. Given an arrow f from A to B, and another arrow g from B to C, their composition is an arrow from A to C. There is also an identity arrow from every object to itself.

For example, Scala forms a category where the objects are Scala types and the arrows are Scala functions. There's another category where the objects are Scala types and the arrows are subtype relationships.

Arrows in a category compose according to certain laws. Composition has to obey an *identity law* such that any arrow f composed with the identity arrow is just f. That is, the identity arrow is *an identity with regard to composition*. Composition also has to obey an *associative law*. Denoting the composition operator as *, the associative law says that (f * g) * h should be the same as f * (g * h). That is, it doesn't matter whether we compose on the left or the right first. This should remind you of the monoid laws!

---

[118]http://en.wikipedia.org/wiki/Category_theory

[119]http://en.wikipedia.org/wiki/Monoid_(category_theory)

[120]http://en.wikipedia.org/wiki/Category_(mathematics)

A `Monoid[M]`, then, is just a category where the only object is the type `M`, and the arrows are the values of type `M`. The identity arrow is the identity element of the monoid, and arrow composition is the monoid's binary operation.

It can be a little difficult to see how the values of a type like `Int` can be *arrows*. Take for instance the monoid formed by integers with addition. Then the integer `5`, say, can be seen as an *operation* that *adds 5* to another integer. And `0` can be seen as an operation that leaves an integer alone.

See Rúnar's article *On Monoids*[121] for some of the deeper connections.

The canonicity of a Scala monoid

In Scala, it's possible to have multiple `Monoid` instances associated with a type. For example, for the type `Int`, we can have a `Monoid[Int]` that uses addition with `0`, and another `Monoid[Int]` that uses multiplication with `1`.

This can lead to certain problems since we cannot count on a `Monoid` instance being *canonical* in any way. To illustrate this problem, consider a "suspended" computation like the following:

```
case class Suspended(acc: Int, m: Monoid[Int], remaining: List[Int])
```

This represents an addition that is "in flight" in some sense. It's an accumulated value so far, represented by `acc`, a monoid `m` that was used to accumulate `acc`, and a list of `remaining` elements to add to the accumulation using the monoid.

Now, if we have *two* values of type `Suspended`, how would we add them together? We have no idea whether the two monoids are the same. And when it comes time to add the two `acc` values, which monoid should we use? There's no way of inspecting the monoids (since they are just functions) to see if they are equivalent. So we have to make an arbitrary guess, or just give up.

Monoids in Haskell[122] work a bit differently. There can only ever be one `Monoid` instance for a given type in Haskell. This is because `Monoid` is a type class[123]. Instances of Haskell *type classes* are not first-class values like they are in Scala. They are implicitly passed and never explicitly referenced. They do not have types per se, but appear as constraints on types[124].

In Haskell, there is only one abstract monoidal operation and one zero. They are both polymorphic, and their signatures are:

```
mappend :: Monoid m => m -> m -> m
mempty  :: Monoid m => m
```

---

[121]http://apocalisp.wordpress.com/2010/06/14/on-monoids/

[122]http://www.haskell.org/haskellwiki/Monoid

[123]https://www.fpcomplete.com/school/starting-with-haskell/introduction-to-haskell/5-type-classes

[124]http://www.haskell.org/tutorial/classes.html

This reads: "for any type m, if m is a monoid, mappend takes an m and another m and returns an m", and "mempty is a value of any type m, given that m is a monoid."

How do we then represent types that are monoids in more than one way, for example Int with addition as one monoid and multiplication as another? The answer is that we make each monoid a newtype[125]:

```
newtype Product = Product { getProduct :: Int }
newtype Sum = Sum { getSum :: Int }
```

A newtype in Haskell is a lot like a case class in Scala, except that newtypes can only have exactly one field, and they have *no runtime representation* other than the underlying type of that field. It's a purely type-level construct, a kind of tagged type.

Using this mechanism, a product and a sum are actually different types, even though the underlying value is an Int in both cases. This way every type has its own canonical monoid, and values accumulated in one monoid can never be confused with values accumulated in another. But we can always convert between them if we need to.

The Scalaz library[126] takes the same approach, where there is only one canonical monoid per type. However, since Scala doesn't have type constraints, the canonicity of monoids is more of a convention than something enforced by the type system. And since Scala doesn't have newtypes, we use phantom types[127] to add tags to the underlying types. This is done with scalaz.Tag[128], which uses a couple of type aliases:

```
type Tagged[A] = AnyRef { type T = A }
type @@[A,B] = A with Tagged[B]
```

Now the type Int @@ Product, for example, is just the type Int, but "tagged" with Product to make it explicit that Monoid[Int @@ Product] is distinct from Monoid[Int @@ Sum]. The types Product and Sum themselves are just empty traits with no members whatsoever.

Tim Perrett wrote a blog post[129] detailing how tagged types work in Scalaz.

The great benefit of canonicity is that Scalaz can build a monoid instance for you just from the type. For example, if you have a Map[Int, Map[String, (Int, Boolean)]], Scalaz can figure out a canonical composite monoid for this type:

---

[125]http://www.haskell.org/haskellwiki/Newtype

[126]https://github.com/scalaz/scalaz

[127]http://www.haskell.org/haskellwiki/Phantom_type

[128]http://docs.typelevel.org/api/scalaz/stable/7.1.0-M3/doc/#scalaz.Tags\protect\char"0024\relax

[129]http://timperrett.com/2012/06/15/unboxed-new-types-within-scalaz7/

```
import scalaz._
import Scalaz._
import Tags._

val x = Map(1 -> Map("Foo" -> (1, Conjunction(false))))
val y = Map(1 -> Map("Foo" -> (2, Conjunction(true))))

val z = x |+| y
```

The value of z will be `Map(1 -> Map("Foo" -> (3, Conjunction(false))))`. Here, `Conjunction` is a "newtype" for `Boolean` to indicate that we want the "conjunction" monoid (`Boolean` with `&&` as the op and `true` as the identity element). There's a corresponding `Disjunction` for `||` with `false`. At the present time, Scalaz's default monoid for `Int` is addition, which is why we get `3` in `z`.

The syntax `x |+| y` works for any monoid. It works because there is an implicit class on the `Scalaz._` import. Be warned though, the `Scalaz._` import brings a lot of implicits into scope. You can import just the monoid syntax with `import scalaz.syntax.monoid._`.

Monoid coproducts

If `A` and `B` are monoids, then `(A,B)` is a monoid, called their *product*. But what about *coproducts*? Is there a composite monoid where we can have *either* an `A` or a `B`? Yes there is. See Rúnar's blog post on monoid coproducts[130] for the details.

Links

On Monoids, by Rúnar[131] – Provides some deeper insight on the relationship between monoids and lists, and looks at them from a category theory perspective.

Notes on chapter 11: Monads

Monad laws through `join`

There is a formulation of the monad laws that we don't discuss in the chapter. We talk about the associative law in terms of `flatMap` and `compose` (Kleisli composition), but we can also state it in terms of `join`:

```
join(join(x)) == join(map(x)(join))
```

---

[130]http://blog.higher-order.com/blog/2014/03/19/monoid-morphisms-products-coproducts/

[131]http://apocalisp.wordpress.com/2010/06/14/on-monoids/

That is, if we have a value x of type F[F[F[A]]], we can join twice to get F[A], or we can map join over the outer F and then join the result of that.

This is saying that in "flattening" F[F[F[A]]] to F[A], it should not matter whether we first join the two "inner" Fs or the two "outer" Fs. This is easy to see with the List monad. If we have a List of Lists of Lists, like this...

```scala
val x: List[List[List[Int]]] =
  List(List(List(1,2), List(3,4)), List(List(5,6), List(7,8)))
```

...it should not matter whether we flatten the inner lists or the outer lists first:

```scala
scala> val y1 = x.flatten
y1: List[List[Int]] = List(List(1, 2), List(3, 4), List(5, 6), List(7, 8))

scala> val y2 = x.map(_.flatten)
y2: List[List[Int]] = List(List(1, 2, 3, 4), List(5, 6, 7, 8))

scala> y1.flatten
res0: List[Int] = List(1, 2, 3, 4, 5, 6, 7, 8)

scala> y2.flatten
res1: List[Int] = List(1, 2, 3, 4, 5, 6, 7, 8)
```

This is the same as saying that in the expression ((1 + 2) + (3 + 4)) + ((5 + 6) + (7 + 8)), it doesn't matter whether we remove the inner brackets first to get (1 + 2 + 3 + 4) + (5 + 6 + 7 + 8) or the outer brackets first to get (1 + 2) + (3 + 4) + (5 + 6) + (7 + 8). In both cases we end up with 1 + 2 + 3 + 4 + 5 + 6 + 7 + 8. The reason it doesn't matter is that + is *associative*. So then it's easy to see how the monad law is an *associative law*.

The identity laws in terms of join are similarly simple:

```scala
join(unit(x)) == x       // left identity
join(map(x)(unit)) == x // right identity
```

In terms of the list monad as above, the identity laws are saying that we can add brackets either on the inside or the outside. Whichever we do, join will behave the same way:

```
scala> val x = List(1,2,3)
x: List[Int] = List(1, 2, 3)

scala> List(x).flatten
res0: List[Int] = List(1, 2, 3)

scala> x.map(List(_)).flatten
res1: List[Int] = List(1, 2, 3)
```

Monads in Category Theory

In Category Theory[132], a Monad[133] is a functor[134] equipped with a pair of natural transformations[135] satisfying the laws of associativity[136] and identity[137].

What does this mean? If we restrict ourselves to the category of Scala types (with Scala types as the objects and functions as the arrows), we can state this in Scala terms.

A `Functor` is just a type constructor for which `map` can be implemented:

```
trait Functor[F[_]] {
  def map[A,B](fa: F[A])(f: A => B): F[B]
}
```

A *natural transformation* from a functor `F` to a functor `G` is just a polymorphic function:

```
trait Transform[F[_], G[_]] {
  def apply[A](fa: F[A]): G[A]
}
```

The natural transformations that form a *monad* for `F` are `unit` and `join`:

---

[132]http://en.wikipedia.org/wiki/Category_theory

[133]http://en.wikipedia.org/wiki/Monad_%28category_theory%29

[134]http://en.wikipedia.org/wiki/Functor

[135]http://en.wikipedia.org/wiki/Natural_transformation

[136]http://en.wikipedia.org/wiki/Associativity

[137]http://en.wikipedia.org/wiki/Identity_%28mathematics%29

```
type Id[A] = A

def unit[F](implicit F: Monad[F]) = new Transform[Id, F] {
  def apply(a: A): F[A] = F.unit(a)
}

def join[F](implicit F: Monad[F]) = new Transform[({type f[x] = F[F[x]]})#f, F] {
  def apply(ffa: F[F[A]]): F[A] = F.join(ffa)
}
```

Monads and monoids

Monoids and monads are connected in various ways in category theory.

The monad for monoids

The `List` monad can be seen as a theory about monoids. Specifically, the `_.flatten` (monadic `join`) and `List(_)` (monadic `unit`) functions witness that we can add and remove parentheses in a monoid expression. That is, the parenthesization of an expression like `1 + 2 + 3 + 4` doesn't matter. The monad associativity law means that we can remove parentheses in any order we like, and the identity law means we can add them wherever we want.

See Rúnar's article, *More on monoids and monads*[138] for more information about this connection.

Kleisli categories

Both monoids and monads form *categories*. In fact, we can see a category as a *generalized monoid*. Observe that with a monoid `M`, we can view each element of the monoid as a function of type `M =>` `M`. For example, in the `Int` monoid with addition, these elements are `(_ + 0)`, `(_ + 1)`, `(_ + (-1))`, etc. Then the composition of these functions is the operation of the monoid. We can generalize this notion to consider not just the type `M`, but all types (`A`, `B`, `C`, etc.) and functions not just of type `M =>` `M`, but `A =>` `B` for any types `A` and `B`. Then ordinary function composition is an associative operation, with an identity element which is the `identity` function that just returns its argument. This more general notion does not form a monoid, but a *category* which is more general. Specifically, it's the *category of Scala types with function composition*. Even more generally, whenever we have *arrows* (a generalized notion of functions) whose composition is associative and has an identity element, we have a category.

A monad `F` can be described by what's called a *Kleisli category*[139]. The objects of this category are the ordinary Scala types, but the arrows are *Kleisli arrows*. That is, every arrow in this category is not of the general form `A =>` `B`, but of the more specific form `A =>` `F[B]`. The composition of these arrows is *Kleisli composition* (given by the `compose` combinator in the chapter) and the identity for Kleisli composition is monadic `unit`. Every monad forms a Kleisli category in this way.

---

[138]http://apocalisp.wordpress.com/2010/07/21/more-on-monoids-and-monads/
[139]http://en.wikipedia.org/wiki/Kleisli_category

A monad is a monoid in a category of endofunctors

A monad is also a kind of monoid. If we think of a type like (M, M) => M as M² => M (taking 2 Ms or the product of M with itself), and M as 1 => M (where 1 is the Unit type), then we can think of a type like F[F[A]] => F[A] as F²[A] => F[A] or just F² ∼> F (where ∼> denotes a natural transformation[140]) and A => F[A] as 1[A] => F[A] (where 1 is the identity functor) or just 1 ∼> F:

type	zero/unit	op/join
Monoid[M]	1 => M	M² => M
Monad[F]	1 ∼> F	F² ∼> F

It's now clear that these are the same kind of thing, except Monoid[M] is operating in a category where the objects are Scala types and the arrows are Scala functions, and Monad[F] is operating in a category where the objects are Scala functors and the arrows are natural transformations.

See this StackOverflow question and its answers: http://stackoverflow.com/questions/3870088/a-monad-is-just-a-monoid-in-the-category-of-endofunctors-whats-the-problem[141].

Reader monad

At the end of the chapter we have an exercise for the reader to implement the following monad:

```scala
case class Reader[R, A](run: R => A)

object Reader {
  def readerMonad[R] = new Monad[({type f[x] = Reader[R,x]})#f] {
    def unit[A](a: => A): Reader[R,A] = ???
    def flatMap[A,B](st: Reader[R,A])(f: A => Reader[R,B]): Reader[R,B] = ???
  }
}
```

This is the reader monad[142]. It is called that because it has the ability to *read* a value of type R. In addition to the operations common to all monads (flatMap, join, map, unit, etc), it has a primitive operation, read:

```scala
def read[R]: Reader[R, R] = Reader(r => r)
```

Note that this is just the identity function!

In the Scalaz library, this operation is called ask[143] and is generalized to any reader-like structure (any implementation of MonadReader) rather than being specific to Reader.

The meaning of map in Reader is function composition:

[140]http://en.wikipedia.org/wiki/Natural_transformation

[141]http://stackoverflow.com/questions/3870088/a-monad-is-just-a-monoid-in-the-category-of-endofunctors-whats-the-problem

[142]http://blog.originate.com/blog/2013/10/21/reader-monad-for-dependency-injection/

[143]http://docs.typelevel.org/api/scalaz/stable/7.1.0-M3/doc/#scalaz.MonadReader

```
def map[R,A,B](f: A => B): Reader[R, A] => Reader[R, B] =
  Reader(r => f compose r.run)
```

The meaning of `join` is to pass the same argument as both parameters to a binary function:

```
def join[R,A](x: Reader[R, Reader[R, A]]): Reader[R, A] =
  Reader(r => x.run(r).run(r))
```

And the meaning of `unit` is to ignore the argument:

```
def unit[R,A](a: A): Reader[R, A] = Reader(_ => a)
```

The reader monad subsumes (and is simpler than) dependency injection[144]. See Rúnar's talks on dependency injection with the reader monad:

"Dead-simple dependency inection", from the 2012 Northeast Scala Symposium in Boston[145]

"Lambda: the ultimate dependency injection framework", from the 2012 YOW! Summer Conference in Brisbane[146]

See also Tony Morris's talk "Dependency injection without the gymnastics"[147] from ETE 2012.

Eilenberg-Moore categories

Another categorical view of monads is through Eilenberg-Moore categories[148]. The EM category of a monad is the category of its algebras[149].

For example, the algebras for the `List` monad are Scala `Monoids`. The EM category of the `List` monad is the category with monoids as its objects and monoid morphisms[150] (see chapter 10) as its arrows.

In general, the EM category for a monad can be found by the following method (source: Theory Lunch[151]):

1. An *F-algebra* for the monad `F` is a type `A` together with a function `a: F[A] => A` such that `a(unit(x)) == x` and `a(join(x)) == a(map(x)(a))`.
2. A morphism of `F`-algebras from an `F`-algebra `a: F[A] => A` to an `F`-algebra `b: F[B] => B` is a function `f: A => B` such that `b(map(x)(f)) == f(a(x))`.

---

[144]http://en.wikipedia.org/wiki/Dependency_injection

[145]https://www.youtube.com/watch?v=ZasXwtTRkio

[146]http://yow.eventer.com/yow-2012-1012/lambda-the-ultimate-dependency-injection-framework-by-runar-bjarnason-1277

[147]http://vimeo.com/44502327

[148]http://ncatlab.org/nlab/show/Eilenberg-Moore+category

[149]https://www.fpcomplete.com/user/bartosz/understanding-algebras

[150]http://en.wikipedia.org/wiki/Monoid#Monoid_homomorphisms

[151]http://theorylunch.wordpress.com/2013/06/06/an-initial-solution-to-the-monad-problem-and-then-some-more/#more-885

3. The Eilenberg-Moore category for the monad `F` is the category with `F`-algebras as objects, and
   morphisms between `F`-algebras as arrows. The identity arrow is just the `identity` function,
   and composition of arrows is ordinary function composition.

We can see how a `Monoid[A]` is precisely a `List`-algebra by this definition:

```scala
def fold[A](implicit M: Monoid[A]): List[A] => A =
  _.foldRight(M.zero)(M.op)
```

It *is* a `List`-algebra because `fold(List(x)) == x` (that is, putting something in a list and then folding
that list is a no-op). And `fold(x.flatten) == fold(x.map(fold.apply))` (that is, concatenating
a bunch of lists and folding the concatenated list is the same as folding a bunch of lists and then
folding the list of the results of those folds).

This is a sense in which "`List` is the monad for monoids."

We can find the EM category for `Option` (thanks, Edward Kmett) easily. Every `Option`-algebra of
type `Option[A] => A` is given by some value `a` of type `A` and is implemented by `_.getOrElse(a)`. So
an object in the EM category for `Option` is a Scala type `A` together with a distinguished value `a:A`.
An arrow in this category takes that value `a:A` to another value `b:B`. So it's a function `f: A => B`
that satisfies `o.map(f).getOrElse(b) == f(o.getOrElse(a))` for all `o: Option[A]`. That is, it's just
a function that returns `b` when given `a`. In other words, `Option` is the monad for *pointed sets*[152].

The EM category for the `Reader[R,_]` or `R => _` monad is the category with objects that are each
given by a value `r:R`, implemented by `_(r)`.

The monad whose EM category is just the category of Scala types is `Id` (the identity monad).

Adjunctions

An *adjunction*[153] consists of a pair of functors in a certain relationship to one another. Stated in
`Scala`, it is an implementation of this interface:

```scala
trait Adjunction[F[_], G[_]] {
  def unit[A](a: A): G[F[A]]
  def counit[A](fga: F[G[A]]): A

  def F: Functor[F]
  def G: Functor[G]
}
```

---

[152]http://en.wikipedia.org/wiki/Pointed_set
[153]http://docs.typelevel.org/api/scalaz/stable/7.1.0-M3/doc/#scalaz.Adjunction

counit is pronounced "co-unit", not "cow-knit".

We say that F is *left adjoint* to G, written $F \dashv G$ in mathematical notation.

There are two laws of adjunctions:

1. `counit(F.map(x)(unit))  ==  x`
2. `G.map(unit(x))(counit)  ==  x`

Another way to view an adjunction is that there is an isomorphism between the types `F[A]  =>  B` and `A  =>  G[B]`:

```
def leftAdjunct[A,B](k: F[A] => B): A => G[B] =
  a => G.map(unit(a))(k)
def rightAdjunct[A,B](k: A => G[B]): F[A] => B =
  fa => counit(F.map(fa)(k))
```

An adjunction has the property that `G[F[_]]` is a monad:

```
def join[A](g: G[F[G[F[A]]]]): G[F[A]] =
  G.map(g)(counit)
def map[A,B](g: G[F[A]])(f: A => B): G[F[B]] =
  G.map(F.map(f))
def flatMap[A,B](g: G[F[A]])(f: A => G[F[B]]): G[F[B]] =
  join(map(g)(f))
```

For example, the `State` monad is formed by the adjoint functors `(_,  S)` and `S  =>  _`.

In fact, *every monad* is formed by an adjunction.

Comonads

Dually[154], the composite functor `F[G[A]]` is a comonad[155]. A comonad is exactly like a monad, except the direction of the function arrows is reversed:

```
trait Comonad[F[_]] {
  def counit[A](a: F[A]): A
  def extend[A,B](a: F[A])(f: F[A] => B): F[B]
}
```

Instead of a `unit` that goes from A to `F[A]`, we have a `counit` that goes from `F[A]` to A. And instead of a `flatMap` that takes a function of type `A  =>  F[B]`, we have `extend` that takes a function going the other way: `F[A]  =>  B`.

A simple example of a comonad is the *reader* comonad:

---

[154]http://en.wikipedia.org/wiki/Dual_%28mathematics%29

[155]http://docs.typelevel.org/api/scalaz/stable/7.1.0-M3/doc/#scalaz.Comonad

```
type Coreader[R,A] = (A,R)

val readerComonad[R] = new Comonad[({type f[x] = Coreader[R,x]})#f] {
  def counit[A](a: (A,R)) = a._1
  def extend[A,B](a: (A,R))(f: (A,R) => B) =
    (f(a), a._2)
}
```

How is this a *reader*? What is it reading? Well, there is a primitive read operation:

```
def read[R](ar: (A,R)): R = ar._2
```

The reader comonad models computations that have a context (or configuration) of type R. The value computed so far is the A, and we can always read the context to copy it into our working memory. It supports the same operations as the reader monad and serves essentially the same purpose.

Note that unlike the reader *monad* which is a function R => A, the reader *comonad* is a pair (A, R). The latter is *left adjoint* to the former and their adjunction forms the State monad.

But their adjunction therefore also forms a comonad! The "dual" of the State monad in this sense is the Store comonad

```
case class Store[S](s: S, f: S => A)
```

The Store comonad essentially models a Moore machine. The current state of the machine is s, and the output function is f. Note that the output depends only on the current state.

The type A => Store[S, A] is one possible representation of a Lens[156].

Other useful comonads include Rose Trees[157], Nonempty lists[158], zippers over lists[159], zippers over trees[160], and cofree comonads[161].

Links

- The essence of functional programming[162] by Philip Wadler.
- Notions of computation and monads[163] by Eugenio Moggi.

---

[156]http://docs.typelevel.org/api/scalaz/stable/7.1.0-M3/doc/#scalaz.package\protect\char"0024\relax\protect\char"0024\relaxLens\protect\char"0024\relax

[157]http://docs.typelevel.org/api/scalaz/stable/7.1.0-M3/doc/#scalaz.Tree

[158]http://docs.typelevel.org/api/scalaz/stable/7.1.0-M3/doc/#scalaz.NonEmptyList

[159]http://docs.typelevel.org/api/scalaz/stable/7.1.0-M3/doc/#scalaz.Zipper

[160]http://docs.typelevel.org/api/scalaz/stable/7.1.0-M3/doc/#scalaz.TreeLoc

[161]http://docs.typelevel.org/api/scalaz/stable/7.1.0-M3/doc/#scalaz.Cofree

[162]http://www.eliza.ch/doc/wadler92essence_of_FP.pdf

[163]http://www.disi.unige.it/person/MoggiE/ftp/ic91.pdf

Notes on chapter 12: Applicative and traversable functors

The cost of power

There is a tradeoff between applicative APIs and monadic ones. Monadic APIs are strictly more powerful and flexible, but the cost is a certain loss of algebraic reasoning.

The difference is easy to demonstrate in theory, but takes some experience to fully appreciate in practice.

Consider composition in a monad, via `compose` (Kleisli composition):

```
val foo: A => F[B] = ???
val bar: B => F[C] = ???
val baz: A => F[C] = bar compose foo
```

There is no way that the implementation of the `compose` function in the `Monad[F]` instance can inspect the values `foo` and `bar`. They are functions, so the only way to "see inside" them is to give them arguments. The values of type `F[B]` and `F[C]` respectively are not determined until the composite function *runs*.

Contrast this with combining values with `map2`:

```
val quux: F[A] = ???
val corge: F[B] = ???
val grault: F[C] = map2(quux, corge)(f)
```

Here the implementation of `map2` can actually look at the values `quux` and `corge`, and take different paths depending on what they are. For instance, it might rewrite them to a normal form for improved efficiency. If F is something like `Future`, it might decide to start immediately evaluating them on different threads. If the data type F is applicative but *not a monad*, then the implementation has this flexibility universally. There is then never any chance that an expression in F is going to involve functions of the form `A => F[B]` that it can't see inside of.

The lesson here is that power and flexibility in the interface often restricts power and flexibility in the implementation. And a more restricted interface often gives the implementation more options.

See this StackOverflow question[164] for a discussion of the issue with regard to parsers.

See also the end of the note below on "Applicative laws", for an example of the loss of algebraic reasoning that comes with making an API monadic rather than applicative.

---

[164] http://stackoverflow.com/questions/7861903/what-are-the-benefits-of-applicative-parsing-over-monadic-parsing

Applicative laws

In the chapter, we decided to present the `Applicative` laws in terms of `map2`. We find that this works pretty well pedagogically. We used the following laws:

- Left identity: `map2(unit(()), fa)((_,a) => a) == fa`
- Right identity: `map2(fa, unit(()))((a,_) => a) == fa`
- Associativity: `product(product(fa, fb),fc) == map(product(fa, product(fb, fc)))(assoc)`
- Naturality: `map2(a,b)(productF(f,g)) == product(map(a)(f), map(b)(g))`

But there are other ways to state the laws for `Applicative`. Commonly the laws for applicative are stated in terms of `apply`, which is sometimes called *idiomatic function application* (where the "idiom" is `F`):

```
def apply[A,B](ff: F[A => B], fa: F[A]): F[B] =
  map2(ff, fa)(_(_))
```

The laws for `apply` are *identity*, *homomorphism*, *interchange*, and *composition*.

Identity law

The identity law for `apply` is stated as:

```
apply(unit(id), v) == v
```

That is, `unit` of the identity function is an identity for `apply`.

Homomorphism law

The homomorphism law for `apply` is stated as:

```
apply(unit(f), unit(x)) == unit(f(x))
```

In other words, idiomatic function application on `unit`s is the same as the `unit` of regular function application. In more precise words, `unit` is a homomorphism from `A` to `F[A]` with regard to function application.

Interchange law

The interchange law for `apply` is stated as:

```
apply(u, unit(y)) == apply(unit(_(y)), u)
```

This law is essentially saying that `unit` is not allowed to carry an effect with regard to any implementation of our applicative functor. If one argument to `apply` is a `unit`, then the other can appear in either position. In other words, it should not matter when we evaluate a `unit`.

Composition

The composition law for `apply` is stated as:

```
apply(u, apply(v, w)) == apply(apply(apply(unit(f => g => f compose g), u), v), w)
```

This is saying that applying `v` to `w` and then applying `u` to that is the same as applying composition to `u`, then `v`, and then applying the composite function to `w`. Intuitively it's saying the same as:

```
u(v(w)) == (u compose v)(w)
```

We might state this law simply as: "function composition in an applicative functor works in the obvious way."

Applicative normal form

The applicative laws taken together can be seen as saying that we can rewrite any expression involving `unit` or `apply` (and therefore by extension `map2`), into a normal form having one of the following shapes:

```
pure(x)          // for some x
map(x)(f)        // for some x and f
map2(x, y)(f)    // for some x, y, and f
map3(x, y, z)(f) // for some x, y, z, and f
// etc.
```

Where f, x, y, and z do not involve the `Applicative` primitives at all. That is, every expression in an applicative functor A can be seen as lifting some pure function f over a number of arguments in A.

Note that this reasoning is lost when the applicative happens to be a monad and the expressions involve `flatMap`. The applicative laws amount to saying that the arguments to `map`, `map2`, `map3`, etc can be reasoned about independently, and an expression like `flatMap(x)(f)` explicitly introduces a dependency (so that the result of f depends on x). See the note above on "The cost of power".

Applicatives in Scalaz

The Scalaz library[165] provides an `Applicative` trait.[166]. In this trait, `map2` et al are called `lift2`, `lift3`, and so on.

The `scalaz.syntax.applicative` object supplies implicit syntax for applicatives to lift a function of arbitrary arity:

```
(x |@| y |@| z)(f)
```

This is equivalent to `lift3(x, y, z)(f)`.

Traversable functors

For further reading on traversable functors, see:

The Essence of the Iterator Pattern[167], by Jeremy Gibbons and Bruno Oliveira. Published in *Mathematically-Structured Functional Programming*, 2006.

Applicative Programming with Effects[168], by Conor McBride and Ross Paterson. Published in *Journal of Functional Programming*, 2008.

An Investigation of the Laws of Traversals[169], by Mauro Jaskelioff and Ondrej Rypacek, published in *Mathematically-Structured Functional Programming*, 2012.

Laws of traversable functors

`Traverse[T[_]]` has two laws. There are many ways to state them, but here is one:

Identity law:

```
sequence[Id,A](xs) == xs
```

That is, traversing in the identity applicative (type `Id[X] = X`) has no effect.

---

[165]http://github.com/scalaz/scalaz

[166]http://docs.typelevel.org/api/scalaz/stable/7.1.0-M3/doc/#scalaz.Applicative

[167]http://web.comlab.ox.ac.uk/oucl/work/jeremy.gibbons/publications/#iterator

[168]http://www.soi.city.ac.uk/~ross/papers/Applicative.html

[169]http://arxiv.org/pdf/1202.2919

Fusion law:

```
sequence[({type f[x] = F[G[x]]})#f, A](xs) ==
  map(sequence[F,G[A]](xs))(sequence[G,A])
```

That is, traversal in `F[_]` followed by traversal in `G[_]` can be fused into one traversal in the composite applicative `F[G[_]]`.

Monad transformers

A *monad transformer* is a data type that composes a particular monad with any other monad, giving us a composite monad that shares the behavior of both.

There is no general way of composing monads. Therefore we have to have a specific transformer for each monad.

For example, `OptionT`[170] is a monad transformer that adds the behavior of `Option` to any other monad. The type `OptionT[M, A]` behaves like the composite monad `M[Option[_]]`. Its `flatMap` method binds over both the `M` and the `Option` inside, saving us from having to do the gymanstics of binding over both.

`Scalaz`[171] provides many more monad transformers, including `StateT`, `WriterT`, `EitherT`, and `ReaderT` (also known as `Kleisli`).

Links

- Applicative Programming with Effects[172]
- The essence of form abstraction[173] talks about writing compositional web forms using applicative functors.
- Brent Yorgey's Typeclassopedia[174] is a great resource on `Monad`, `Applicative`, `Traverse` and other type classes.

Notes on chapter 13: External effects and I/O

Monads were discovered as a way of embedding effectful code into a pure language in the early 1990s–see the 1992 Phillip Wadler paper The essence of functional programming[175] and also

---

[170]http://docs.typelevel.org/api/scalaz/stable/7.1.0-M3/doc/#scalaz.OptionT

[171]http://github.com/scalaz/scalaz

[172]http://www.soi.city.ac.uk/~ross/papers/Applicative.html

[173]http://groups.inf.ed.ac.uk/links/formlets/

[174]http://www.haskell.org/haskellwiki/Typeclassopedia

[175]http://homepages.inf.ed.ac.uk/wadler/papers/essence/essence.ps

Imperative functional programming[176] by Simon Peyton Jones (one of the creators of Haskell) and Wadler.

There are various ways of representing the `Free` data type we made use of here. The traditional formulation would be in terms of just two constructors, `Return` and `Suspend`:

```scala
trait Free[F[_],A]
case class Return[F[_],A](a: A) extends Free[F,A]
case class Suspend[F[_],A](f: F[Free[F, A]]) extends Free[F,A]
```

This type forms a `Monad` given only a `Functor[F]`. See Free Monads and the Yoneda Lemma[177] which talks about the relationship between these various formulations of `Free` and introduces some relevant category theory.

Performance of `Free`

The naive, two-constructor representation of `Free` above has quadratic complexity for left-associated sequences of `flatMap` (more standard terminology is "bind" rather than `flatMap`). For example:

```scala
def f(i: Int): Free[F,Int] = ...
val acc: Free[F,Int] = ...

val bad = (0 until N).map(f).foldLeft(acc)(_.map2(_)(_ + _))
```

This requires repeated trips to the "end" of the increasingly long chain to attach a further `map2`. The first iteration requires 1 step, the next requires 2 steps, then 3 steps, and so on, up to N, leading to quadratic complexity. See Reflection without remorse[178] which gives a very nice overview of the general problem, discusses historical solutions and their tradeoffs, and presents a new solution based on *type-aligned sequences*. Our solution given in the text rewrites binds to the right during interpretation in the `runFree` function[179], which assumes that the target `Monad` has efficient implementation for right-associated binds.

Lack of first-class universal quantification in Scala

The `Translate` type we introduced in this chapter is a common idiom for getting around Scala's lack of support for *first-class, universally quantified values*. We'd like for `runFree` to just accept a `forall A . F[A] => G[A]` (this is not valid Scala syntax), but first-class functions and in fact all first-class values in Scala are monomorphic–any type parameters they mention must be fixed to some particular types. To get around this restriction, we defined `Translate[F,G]`:

---

[176]http://homepages.inf.ed.ac.uk/wadler/papers/imperative/imperative.ps

[177]http://blog.higher-order.com/blog/2013/11/01/free-and-yoneda/

[178]http://homepages.cwi.nl/~ploeg/papers/zseq.pdf

[179]https://github.com/fpinscala/fpinscala/blob/master/answers/src/main/scala/fpinscala/iomonad/IO.scala#L419

```
trait Translate[F[_],G[_]] {
  def apply[A](f: F[A]): G[A]
}
```

Although values must be monomorphic, *methods* in Scala can of course be polymorphic, so we simply introduce a new first-class type containing a polymorphic method. Unfortunately, this means that various polymorphic methods we might have lying around must be explicitly wrapped in Translate:

```
def headOption[A](a: List[A]): Option[A]
```

Even though headOption is polymorphic, we would need to explicitly wrap it in a Translate[List,Option] if we ever needed to use it polymorphically in a first-class way. Another drawback of this approach is that we require separate versions of Translate for different "shapes" of the input and output type constructors–for instance, in chapter 14, we define a type RunnableST, which would typically just be represented using a universally quantified ordinary value, without needing wrapping in a new type.

Links

See Free Monads and Free Monoids[180] for more information about what "free" means.

Notes on chapter 14: Local effects and mutable state

The ST data type covered in this chapter was first introduced in Lazy Functional State Threads[181]. The general idea, of using universal quantification to uniquely tag variables and enforce scoping, is also useful in other situations. For instance, we can use the same idea to enforce a 'safe' API for accessing file handles, preventing a file handle from being referenced after it passes out of scope. Here is a sketch of an API:

---

[180]http://blog.higher-order.com/blog/2013/08/20/free-monads-and-free-monoids/
[181]http://citeseerx.ist.psu.edu/viewdoc/summary?doi=10.1.1.50.3299

```
trait Handle[R]

trait SafeIO[S,+A] {
  def flatMap[B](f: A => SafeIO[S,B]): SafeIO[S,B]
  def map[B](f: A => B): SafeIO[S,B]
}

object SafeIO {
  def unit[S,A](a: A): SafeIO[S,A]

  // obtain a file handle
  def handle[S](filename: String): SafeIO[S, Handle[S]]

  // read a number of bytes from a handle, safely
  def read[S](h: Handle[S], n: Int): SafeIO[S, Option[Array[Byte]]]

  // run a 'closed' `SafeIO` computation
  def run[A](io: RunIO[A]): IO[A]
}

/** A 'runnable' `SafeIO` must be universally quantified in `S`. */
trait RunIO[A] { def run[S]: SafeIO[S,A] }
```

By tagging Handle values with the scope in which they originate, we prevent running a SafeIO whose value incorporates a Handle, and we are also prevented from mixing Handle values originating in different scopes. Thus, any Handle values allocated during run may be safely closed when the IO action returned from run completes.

In many situations where we might use universal quantification like this to enforce some notion of scoping, we can alternately "invert control". For instance, the need to enforce scoping in both SafeIO (and ST) comes about because we allow access to an underlying "handle" concept (for ST, we have STRef and STArray, which are handles to mutable references), and we want to ensure that these handles pass out of scope at some delimited location. We can instead choose to work with a different abstraction not based on handles at all. Rather than letting the computation pull data from a Handle, we can instead build up a "transducer" that gives abstract instructions for how to transform one input stream to another, without getting access to any underlying handle. For instance, the library we develop in chapter 15 provides access to files but the various consumers of our Process type don't deal directly with a Handle abstraction.

Effect systems

Universal quantification is a very simple technique for enforcing effect scoping, and the ST type is easy to incorporate as a regular library into many functional languages. There are more sophisticated techniques for tracking effects, called *effect systems*. The general idea here is that we track the *effects* of a value separate from its type. Effect systems often include natural subtyping of effects, so that, for instance, a pure computation (with no effects) can be passed as an argument without explicit wrapping to a function allowing for the effect of mutation to some variable or region of memory. See for example Koka[182], DDC[183], and Frank[184].

Notes on chapter 15: Stream processing and incremental I/O

As mentioned in the text, an I/O monad is a kind of lowest common denominator for embedding externally-interpreted effects in a pure language–the model when programming *within* IO is much the same as ordinary imperative programming. Hence, ever since the IO monad was first introduced in the early 1990s, functional programmers have been interested in finding more compositional ways of assembling programs that talk to the external world.

For a while, lazy I/O was still quite commonly used, despite its problems. Oleg Kiselyov, a prominent Haskell programmer and researcher, was very vocal in pointing out the problems with lazy I/O[185], and popularized the concept of *iteratees*, which is an early "ancestor" of the library we developed in this chapter. For more background, see Oleg's page on stream processing[186]. For a gentler exposition to iteratees, also see "Iteratee: Teaching an old fold new tricks" in Issue 16 of The Monad Reader[187]. Oleg's site[188] is a treasure trove of resources covering various aspects of FP, we highly recommend spending some time there.

In the past 5 years or so, there have been a number of variations developed on the basic idea of iteratees, generally aimed at making simpler to use and/or more expressive libraries. In Haskell, see the conduit[189] and pipes[190] packages, as well as Edward Kmett's machines[191] package, which is the Haskell library which most closely related to the one in this chapter.

There's been some pushback in the Haskell community that the conduit and pipes packages are overly complicated, and this has led to the development of the io-streams[192] package. The library is simpler in the sense that it is specialized to IO and bakes certain features directly into the basic stream types used, but in our opinion, this library isn't really a full replacement for a library like conduit, pipes, or machines. An important goal of a stream processing library is to allow for pure stream processing logic (often a majority of processing logic) to be defined separately from any I/O. Although having

---

[182]http://www.rise4fun.com/koka/tutorial

[183]http://www.haskell.org/haskellwiki/DDC

[184]http://cs.ioc.ee/efftt/mcbride-slides.pdf

[185]http://okmij.org/ftp/Haskell/Iteratee/Lazy-vs-correct.txt

[186]http://okmij.org/ftp/Streams.html

[187]http://themonadreader.files.wordpress.com/2010/05/issue16.pdf

[188]http://okmij.org/ftp/

[189]https://www.fpcomplete.com/user/snoyberg/library-documentation/conduit-overview

[190]https://hackage.haskell.org/package/pipes-4.1.2/docs/Pipes-Tutorial.html

[191]https://hackage.haskell.org/package/machines

[192]http://hackage.haskell.org/package/io-streams-1.0.1.0/docs/System-IO-Streams-Tutorial.html

a more convenient abstraction for I/O streams is useful, more general purpose, abstract libraries are still important.

In the Scala world, the scalaz-stream library[193] developed out of work on machines[194] and the library developed here. Prior to that, there were ports of iteratees in the core scalaz library[195].

Functional reactive programming

Streaming processing and incremental I/O might not seem to have much to do with UI programming, but the problems have similarities. Functional Reactive Programming[196] (FRP) originated in the 1990s with work done by Conal Elliott[197], Paul Hudak, and others (see Elliott's list of publications[198] and the 1997 paper Functional Reactive Animation[199] by Elliott and Hudak). FRP is often put forward as a solution to the problem of describing interactive UIs in a functional way.

The FRP research has developed somewhat in parallel to the various approaches to streaming I/O mentioned above. According to Elliott, what uniquely identifies FRP is the use of *continuous time*[200], and on providing a simple, precise *denotation* for the data types and various combinators. An FRP library is based around two types of signals:

- `Behavior[A]`: a time-varying A value, having a denotation `Time => A`.
- `Event[A]`: a discrete, time-varying sequence of A values, having a denotation of `List (Time, A)`.

These types (and their denotations) are deliberately abstract, which means that implementations are free to expose different sets of primitive combinators, and implementations are free to use very different implementation strategies, depending on what primitives are exposed to users. See the chapter notes for chapter 9[201] for more about this style of design. For instance, the algebra might include the following functions:

- `def foldP[B,A](e: Event[A], z: B)(f: (B,A) => B): Event[B]` for left-folding the sequence of values represented by an `Event`.
- `def sample[A,B](e: Event[A], b: Behavior[B]): Event[B]` for sampling from a continuous behavior whenever an `Event` emits a value

[193]https://github.com/scalaz/scalaz-stream

[194]https://hackage.haskell.org/package/machines

[195]https://github.com/scalaz/scalaz

[196]http://en.wikipedia.org/wiki/Functional_reactive_programming

[197]http://conal.net/

[198]http://conal.net/papers/

[199]http://conal.net/papers/icfp97/

[200]http://conal.net/blog/posts/why-program-with-continuous-time

[201]Chapter-9:-Parser-combinators

Each of these operations can be given a clear interpretation in terms of the denotations of `Event` and `Behavior`, but implementations may use some more interesting representation of these types to facilitate efficient interpretation.

The FRP use of continuous time is important for much the same reasons that non-strictness is important. We saw in chapter 5 how non-strictness let us write more modular code, by decoupling the description of a computation (which may be infinite) from its evaluation. In the same way, continuous time lets us decouple the description of a time-varying program from any *sampling* or *discretization* that occurs at the end of the day when running our program.

In some ways, the denotations for `Event` and `Behavior` are a little *too* flexible–there is no enforcement of *causality*, for instance–a `Behavior[A] => Behavior[B]` could in priciple let the value of the output behavior at time *t* depend on the value of the input behavior at time *t + k*, essentially "looking into the future" to determine the value at the present. Elliott discusses some of these problems in this post[202]. The flexibility of the semantic model also means it is not immediately clear what actual algebra should be exposed to the programmer–we clearly want something expressive, but also limited "in the right ways" such that it is possible to implement efficiently. This is a challenging design problem in and of itself.

FRP is a deep area within functional programming. Here are just a few links to learn more:

- Push-pull FRP[203] by Elliott provides a nice, modern introduction to the ideas of FRP and discusses issues in crafting an efficient implementation. We also like Heinrich Apfelmus' blog[204], which has a number of posts talking about FRP and various implementation issues.
- *Arrowized FRP (AFRP)* arose in part because of the difficulties in formulating efficient implementations of the FRP model. In AFRP, behaviors and events are not first class, instead we have first-class signal transformers, generally based on some variation of the `Arrow` algebra. See The Reactive Arcade[205], which has an introduction to Yampa, an AFRP system, and also Causal Commutative Arrows and their Optimization[206], which discusses ways of optimizing AFRP for efficient implementation.
- With both arrowized and traditional FRP, there are questions about the best way to allow for various forms of context-sensitivity and dynamic switching between signals (sometimes called "dynamic event switching"). The need for this can arise in many situations, but, for instance, it can be used for modeling UIs in which the user can add and remove new UI elements by interacting with existing UI elements on the page. In traditional FRP, use of dynamic event switching can make it easy to introduce *time leaks*, due to accidentally retaining the full history of an `Event`–Heinrich Apfelmus discusses this issue here[207]. And in AFRP, since the signals themselves are not first class, it isn't immediately obvious what the best way is to represent and interact with a dynamic, changing set of signals (though this issue has been

---

[202]http://conal.net/blog/posts/garbage-collecting-the-semantics-of-frp

[203]http://conal.net/papers/push-pull-frp/

[204]http://apfelmus.nfshost.com/blog.html

[205]http://www.antonycourtney.com/pubs/hw03.pdf

[206]http://cs-www.cs.yale.edu/c2/images/uploads/ICFP-CCA.pdf

[207]http://apfelmus.nfshost.com/blog/2011/05/15-frp-dynamic-event-switching.html

also addressed in the AFRP line of research, see Antony Courtney's thesis[208] pg 123, also the Reactive Arcade[209] and FRP, continued[210] papers).

Over time, the term "FRP" has been somewhat diluted, and the term is sometimes incorrectly used to refer to systems with discrete time, and even decidedly non-functional libraries making use of explicit callbacks and side effects!

---

[208]http://www.antonycourtney.com/pubs/ac-thesis.pdf

[209]http://www.antonycourtney.com/pubs/hw03.pdf

[210]http://haskell.cs.yale.edu/wp-content/uploads/2011/02/workshop-02.pdf

Hints for exercises

This section contains hints for various exercises in the book, to help you get started in coming up with an answer, or to get you unstuck if you run into trouble.

Not all exercises have hints. If you think of a good hint for an exercise and would like it to be available to other readers, submit a pull request to the book's GitHub repository.[211] The electronic version of these hints is available under the answerkey directory in that repository.

Hints for exercises in chapter 2

Exercise 2.01

You will definitely need a helper method like we did with factorial. But think about what information you need at each iteration. You might need two values, one for each of the two numbers you need to calculate the next number. And you know the first two numbers already.

Note that the nth Fibonacci number has a closed form solution (see http://en.wikipedia.org/wiki/Fibonacci_number#Closed-form_expression). Using that would be cheating; the point here is just to get some practice writing loops with tail-recursive functions.

Exercise 2.02

You know the array is not sorted as soon as you encounter two adjacent elements for which gt(first, second) returns true (note that equal adjacent elements are in order).

Exercise 2.03

You have to take an argument of type A and return a function of type B => C. That function has to take an argument of type B and return a value of type C. Follow the types.

Exercise 2.04

You want to return a binary function, so start by taking two arguments. You will have to pass those arguments to f one at a time.

---

[211]https://github.com/fpinscala/fpinscala

Exercise 2.05

You need to return a new function of type A => C. Start by accepting an argument of type A. Now follow the types. You have an A. What can you do with it? Do you have a function that accepts an A?

Hints for exercises in chapter 3

Exercise 3.02

Try pattern matching on l.

Exercise 3.04

What should the function do if the n argument is 0? What should it do if the list is empty? What if the list is not empty and n is nonzero? Consider all of these cases. Use pattern-matching and recursion.

Exercise 3.05

What should the function do if the list is empty? What if it's not empty? Use pattern-matching and recursion.

Exercise 3.07

Look at the program trace from the previous example. Based on the trace, is it possible the function supplied could choose to terminate the recursion early?

Exercise 3.08

The first step in the trace is Cons(1, foldRight(Cons(2, Cons(3, Nil)), Nil:List[Int])(Cons(_-,_)))

Exercise 3.13

It's possible to do both directions. For your foldLeft in terms of foldRight, you must build up, using foldRight, some value that you can use to achieve the effect of foldLeft. (It won't be the B of the return type necessarily)

Exercise 3.15

Use foldRight.

Exercise 3.16

Try using `foldRight`. You shouldn't need to resort to an explicitly recursive function.

Exercise 3.17

Again, try using `foldRight`. You shouldn't need to resort to an explicitly recursive function.

Exercise 3.18

Again, try using `foldRight`. You shouldn't need to resort to an explicitly recursive function.

Exercise 3.19

Again, try using `foldRight`!

Exercise 3.20

You should be able to use a combination of existing functions.

Exercise 3.24

It's good to specify some properties about your implementation up front. For example, do you expect these expressions to be true?

```
(xs append ys append zs) hasSubsequence ys
```

```
xs hasSubsequence Nil
```

You will find that the answer to one of these implies something about the other.

Exercise 3.28

The signature is `def map[A,B](t: Tree[A])(f: A => B): Tree[B]`.

Exercise 3.29

The signature is `def fold[A,B](t: Tree[A])(l: A => B)(b: (B,B) => B): B`. See if you can define this function, then reimplement the functions you've already written for `Tree`.

Hints for exercises in chapter 4

Exercise 4.03

Use the flatMap and possibly map methods.

Exercise 4.04

Break the list out using pattern-matching where there will be a recursive call to sequence in the cons case. Alternatively, use the foldRight method to take care of the recursion for you.

Exercise 4.05

The traverse function can be written with explicit recursion or use foldRight to do the recursion for you. Implementing sequence using traverse may be more trivial than you think.

Exercise 4.06

The map2 function that we wrote earlier for Option will follow the same pattern for Either.

Exercise 4.07

The signature of traverse is

```
def traverse[E,A,B](es: List[A])(f: A => Either[E, B]): Either[E, List[B]]
```

And the signature of sequence is:

```
def sequence[E,A](es: List[Either[E, A]]): Either[E, List[A]]
```

In your implementation, you can pattern-match the list and use explicit recursion or use foldRight to perform the recursion for you.

Hints for exercises in chapter 5

Exercise 5.02

Many Stream functions can start by pattern matching on the Stream and considering what to do in each of the two cases. This particular function needs to first consider whether it needs to look at the stream at all.

Exercise 5.04

Use foldRight.

Exercise 5.06

Let None: Option[A] be the first argument to foldRight. Follow the types from there.

Exercise 5.09

The example function ones is recursive. How could you define from recursively?

Exercise 5.10

Chapter two discussed writing loops functionally, using a recursive helper function. How would that apply here?

Exercise 5.11

Review the techniques you used in exercise 4.1 for working with Option.

Exercise 5.14

Try to avoid using explicit recursion. Use zipAll and takeWhile.

Exercise 5.15

Try unfold with this as the starting state. You may want to handle emitting the empty Stream at the end as a special case.

Exercise 5.16

The function can't be implemented using unfold, since unfold generates elements of the Stream from left to right. It can be implemented using foldRight though.

Hints for exercises in chapter 6

Exercise 6.02

Use nonNegativeInt to generate a random integer between 0 and Int.MaxValue, inclusive. Then map that to the range of doubles from 0 to 1.

Exercise 6.05

This is an application of `map` over `nonNegativeInt` or `nextInt`.

Exercise 6.06

Start by accepting an RNG. Note that you have a choice in which RNG to pass to which function, and in what order. Think about what you expect the behavior to be, and whether your implementation meets that expectation.

Exercise 6.07

You need to recursively iterate over the list. Remember that you can use `foldLeft` or `foldRight` instead of writing a recursive definition. You can also reuse the `map2` function you just wrote. As a test case for your implementation, we should expect `sequence(List(unit(1), unit(2), unit(3)))(r)._1` to return `List(1, 2, 3)`.

Exercise 6.08

The implementation using `flatMap` will be almost identical to the failed one where we tried to use `map`.

Exercise 6.10

Use the specialized functions for `Rand` as inspiration.

Hints for exercises in chapter 7

Exercise 7.01

The function shouldn't require that the two `Par` inputs have the same type.

Exercise 7.02

What if `run` were backed by a `java.util.concurrent.ExecutorService`? You may want to spend some time looking through the `java.util.concurrent` package to see what other useful things you can find.

Exercise 7.03

In order to respect timeouts, we'd need a new `Future` implementation that records the amount of time spent evaluating one future, then subtracts that time from the available time allocated for evaluating the other future.

Exercise 7.05

One possible implementation will be very similar in structure to a function we've implemented previously, for `Option`.

Exercise 7.08

There is a problem is with fixed size thread pools. What happens if the thread pool is bounded to be of exactly size 1?

Exercise 7.10

Try adding a second continuation argument to `Future.apply`, which takes an error handler.

Hints for exercises in chapter 8

Exercise 8.01

When thinking of properties a function should satisfy, it often helps to consider inputs that have some structure that is easy to describe. A list where all the elements are the same is one simple structure.

Exercise 8.03

We can refer to the enclosing `Prop` instance with `Prop.this`

Exercise 8.12

Use the `listOfN` function you wrote before.

Exercise 8.13

You can use a sized generator.

Exercise 8.15

You will need to add to the representation of Gen. For example, Gen[Int] should be capable of generating random integers as well as generating a stream of all the integers from Int.MinValue to Int.MaxValue. You may want to have the behavior depend on how many test cases were requested.

Exercise 8.17

Use the Gen[Par[Int]] generator from the last exercise.

Exercise 8.19

If we are just looking at the random case, one way to have the generated Int depend on the String might be to set the seed of a new random number generator to be equal to the hashCode of the given input String.

Exercise 8.22

Use the Gen[Par[Int]] generator from the last exercise.

Exercise 8.25

If we are just looking at the random case, one way to have the generated Int depend on the String might be to set the seed of a new random number generator to be equal to the hashCode of the given input String.

Hints for exercises in chapter 9

Exercise 9.01

Try mapping over the result of product.

Exercise 9.02

Multiplication of numbers is associative, a * (b * c) == (a * b) * c. Is there an analogous property for parsers? What can you say about the relationship between map and product?

Exercise 9.06

Given a string of digits, s, you can use s.toInt to convert that to an Int.

Exercise 9.07

Use `flatMap` and `succeed`.

Exercise 9.09

For the tokens of your grammar, it's often a good idea to skip any trailing whitespace, to avoid having to deal with whitespace everywhere in your grammar. Try introducing a combinator for this.

When sequencing parsers with **, it's common to want to ignore one of the parsers in the sequence, and you'll probably want to introduce combinators for this.

Exercise 9.11

Here are two options: we could return the most recent error in the or chain, or we could return whichever error occurred after getting furthest into the input string.

Exercise 9.14

You may want `string` to report the immediate cause of failure (whichever character didn't match), as well as the overall string being parsed.

Exercise 9.17

Try adding another piece of state to `Location`, `isSliced`. You may want to rename `Location` to `ParseState`, as it's no longer just the location!

Exercise 9.18

You can add an attribute `otherFailures: List[ParseError]` on `ParseError` itself. This will be a list of parse errors that occurred in other branches of the parser.

Hints for exercises in chapter 10

Exercise 10.02

Because we are abstract in the type parameter A, we are limited in the number of possible implementations. But there's more than one implementation that meets the monoid laws.

Exercise 10.03

Again we are limited in the number of ways we can combine values with op since it should compose functions of type A => A for *any* choice of A. And again there is more than one possible implementation. There is only one possible zero though.

Exercise 10.04

You will need to generate three values of type A for testing associativity. Write a new Gen combinator for this if necessary.

Exercise 10.05

You can map and then concatenate, but that will go over the list twice. Use a single fold instead.

Exercise 10.06

Notice that the type of the function that is passed to foldRight is (A, B) => B, which can be curried to A => (B => B). This is a strong hint that we should use the endofunction monoid B => B to implement foldRight. The implementation of foldLeft is then just the dual. Don't worry if these implementations are not very efficient.

Exercise 10.07

The sequences of lengths 0 and 1 are special cases to consider.

Exercise 10.08

Think about what a partial answer looks like. If we've only seen some of the elements of a sequence, we need to know if what we have seen so far is ordered. For every new element we see, if the sequence is in fact ordered, it should not fall inside the range of elements seen already.

Exercise 10.09

Try creating a data type which tracks the *interval* of the values in a given segment, as well as whether an "unordered segment" has been found.

When merging the values for two segments, think about how these two pieces of information should be updated.

Exercise 10.10

A `Stub` should never contain any whitespace.

Exercise 10.11

You can write default implementations on the `Foldable` trait an then `override` them as necessary.

Exercise 10.18

Use `mapMergeMonoid` and `intAddition`.

Hints for exercises in chapter 11

Exercise 11.01

You have already defined `unit` and `flatMap` for these types. The solution is to simply call them from your `Monad` implementation.

Exercise 11.02

Since `State` is a binary type constructor, we need to partially apply it with the `S` type argument. Thus, it is not just one monad, but an entire family of monads, one for each type `S`. You need to devise a way of capturing the type `S` in a type-level scope and providing a partially applied `State` type in that scope.

Exercise 11.03

These implementations should be very similar to implementations from previous chapters, only with more general types, and using the functions on the `Monad` trait. Make use of `unit` and `map2`.

Exercise 11.04

There is more than one way of writing this function. For example, try starting with a `List[F[A]]` of length `n`.

Exercise 11.06

You can start by pattern matching on the argument. If the list is empty, our only choice is to return `unit(Nil)`

Exercise 11.07

Follow the types. There is only one possible implementation.

Exercise 11.08

Look at the signature of compose. What happens if A is Unit?

Exercise 11.09

You want to show that these two are equivalent:

```
flatMap(flatMap(x)(f))(g) == flatMap(x)(a => flatMap(f(a))(g))
```

```
compose(compose(f, g), h) == compose(f, compose(g, h))
```

Rewrite one in terms of the other.

Exercise 11.12

Follow the types here. Remember that A can be *any type at all*, including the type F[B] for some type B.

Exercise 11.13

Join is sometimes called "flatten", and flatMap "maps and then flattens".

Exercise 11.14

Rewrite the monad laws stated in terms of flatMap by substituting your implementation of join.

Exercise 11.19

What would you expect getState to return right after you call setState?

Exercise 11.20

This monad is very similar to the State monad, except that it's "read-only". You can "get" but not "set" the R value that flatMap carries along.

Hints for exercises in chapter 12

Exercise 12.02

To implement map2 in terms of apply, try using f.curried and following the types.

Exercise 12.03

Look at your implementation of map2 in terms of apply and try to follow the same pattern.

Exercise 12.04

Try it yourself in the REPL with some small examples.

Exercise 12.05

You can write flatMap using pattern matching.

Exercise 12.06

Implement map2 using pattern matching. If both sides are a failure, try to keep the order of failures consistent.

Exercise 12.07

Implement map2 in terms of flatMap. Start with each applicative law in turn, then substitute equals for equals and apply the monad laws until you get an equation that is obviously true.

Exercise 12.08

Follow the types.

Exercise 12.09

The definition of map2 is very short. The only things you can do are map2 and unit from the F and G applicatives. Follow the types.

Exercise 12.10

You will find this very difficult without an interactive proof assistant like Coq or Agda. If you do decide to take on the challenge, this is the kind of problem that might take someone several days or even a few weeks to think about.

Exercise 12.12

The standard library lets you treat a `Map` as essentially a list of pairs.

Exercise 12.13

Follow the types. There is generally only one sensible implementation that typechecks.

Exercise 12.14

What happens if you call `traverse` with `Applicative[Option]`? Is there an even simpler `Applicative` you could use?

Exercise 12.16

We need to use a stack. Fortunately a `List` is the same thing as a stack, and we already know how to turn any traversable into a list!

Exercise 12.17

This implementation is very similar to `toList` except instead of accumulating into a list, we are accumulating into a `B` using the `f` function.

Exercise 12.19

Follow the types. There is only implementation that typechecks.

Exercise 12.20

Follow the types. There is only implementation that typechecks.

Hints for exercises in chapter 13

Exercise 13.02

Pattern this after the TailRec interpreter we gave in the text earlier

Exercise 13.04

To define translate, use `runFree` with `Free[Function0,_]` as the target monad. Then use the specialized `runTrampoline` function written earlier.

Exercise 13.05

Use `Par.async[Either[Throwable,Array[Byte]]] { cb => ... }`. Follow the types - what is the type of `cb` here and how can you use it?

Hints for exercises in chapter 15

Exercise 15.03

You'll need to use a local helper function which accepts the current sum and count.

Exercise 15.11

Use `await`

Answers to exercises

This section contains answers to exercises in the book. Note that usually only one answer is given per exercise, but there may be more than one correct answer. We highly recommend that you check out the book's source code repository from GitHub[212] and look at the answers given there for each chapter. Those answers are shown *in context*, with more detailed explanations, more varied solutions, and in some cases complete implementations that do not fit in this booklet.

Answers to exercises for chapter 2

Exercise 2.01

```scala
def fib(n: Int): Int = {
  @annotation.tailrec
  def loop(n: Int, prev: Int, cur: Int): Int =
    if (n == 0) prev
    else loop(n - 1, cur, prev + cur)
  loop(n, 0, 1)
}
```

0 and 1 are the first two numbers in the sequence, so we start the accumulators with those. At every iteration, we add the two numbers to get the next one.

Exercise 2.02

```scala
def isSorted[A](as: Array[A], gt: (A,A) => Boolean): Boolean = {
  @annotation.tailrec
  def go(n: Int): Boolean =
    if (n >= as.length-1) true
    else if (gt(as(n), as(n+1))) false
    else go(n+1)

  go(0)
}
```

Exercise 2.03

Note that => associates to the right, so we could write the return type as A => B => C

---

[212]https://github.com/fpinscala/fpinscala

```scala
def curry[A,B,C](f: (A, B) => C): A => (B => C) =
  a => b => f(a, b)
```

NB: The Function2 trait has a curried method already, so if you wanted to cheat a little you could write the answer as f.curried

Exercise 2.04

```scala
def uncurry[A,B,C](f: A => B => C): (A, B) => C =
  (a, b) => f(a)(b)
```

NB: There is a method on the Function object in the standard library, Function.uncurried that you can use for uncurrying.

Note that we can go back and forth between the two forms. We can curry and uncurry and the two forms are in some sense "the same". In FP jargon, we say that they are *isomorphic* ("iso" = same; "morphe" = shape, form), a term we inherit from category theory.

Exercise 2.05

```scala
def compose[A,B,C](f: B => C, g: A => B): A => C =
  a => f(g(a))
```

Answers to exercises for chapter 3

Exercise 3.01

Three. The third case is the first that matches, with x bound to 1 and y bound to 2.

Exercise 3.02

Although we could return Nil when the input list is empty, we choose to throw an exception instead. This is a somewhat subjective choice. In our experience, taking the tail of an empty list is often a bug, and silently returning a value just means this bug will be discovered later, further from the place where it was introduced.

It's generally good practice when pattern matching to use _ for any variables you don't intend to use on the right hand side of a pattern. This makes it clear the value isn't relevant.

```
def tail[A](l: List[A]): List[A] =
  l match {
    case Nil => sys.error("tail of empty list")
    case Cons(_,t) => t
  }
```

Exercise 3.03

If a function body consists solely of a match expression, we'll often put the match on the same line as the function signature, rather than introducing another level of nesting.

```
def setHead[A](l: List[A], h: A): List[A] = l match {
  case Nil => sys.error("setHead on empty list")
  case Cons(_,t) => Cons(h,t)
}
```

Exercise 3.04

Again, it's somewhat subjective whether to throw an exception when asked to drop more elements than the list contains. The usual default for drop is not to throw an exception, since it's typically used in cases where this is not indicative of a programming error. If you pay attention to how you use drop, it's often in cases where the length of the input list is unknown, and the number of elements to be dropped is being computed from something else. If drop threw an exception, we'd have to first compute or check the length and only drop up to that many elements.

```
def drop[A](l: List[A], n: Int): List[A] =
  if (n <= 0) l
  else l match {
    case Nil => Nil
    case Cons(_,t) => drop(t, n-1)
  }
```

Exercise 3.05

Somewhat overkill, but to illustrate the feature we're using a *pattern guard*, to only match a Cons whose head satisfies our predicate, f. The syntax is to add if <cond> after the pattern, before the =>, where <cond> can use any of the variables introduced by the pattern.

```
def dropWhile[A](l: List[A], f: A => Boolean): List[A] =
  l match {
    case Cons(h,t) if f(h) => dropWhile(t, f)
    case _ => l
  }
```

Exercise 3.06

Note that we're copying the entire list up until the last element. Besides being inefficient, the natural recursive solution will use a stack frame for each element of the list, which can lead to stack overflows for large lists (can you see why?). With lists, it's common to use a temporary, mutable buffer internal to the function (with lazy lists or streams, which we discuss in chapter 5, we don't normally do this). So long as the buffer is allocated internal to the function, the mutation is not observable and RT is preserved.

Another common convention is to accumulate the output list in reverse order, then reverse it at the end, which doesn't require even local mutation. We'll write a reverse function later in this chapter.

```
def init[A](l: List[A]): List[A] =
  l match {
    case Nil => sys.error("init of empty list")
    case Cons(_,Nil) => Nil
    case Cons(h,t) => Cons(h,init(t))
  }
def init2[A](l: List[A]): List[A] = {
  import collection.mutable.ListBuffer
  val buf = new ListBuffer[A]
  @annotation.tailrec
  def go(cur: List[A]): List[A] = cur match {
    case Nil => sys.error("init of empty list")
    case Cons(_,Nil) => List(buf.toList: _*)
    case Cons(h,t) => buf += h; go(t)
  }
  go(l)
}
```

Exercise 3.07

No, this is not possible! The reason is because *before* we ever call our function, f, we evaluate its argument, which in the case of foldRight means traversing the list all the way to the end. We need *non-strict* evaluation to support early termination—we discuss this in chapter 5.

Exercise 3.08

We get back the original list! Why is that? As we mentioned earlier, one way of thinking about what foldRight "does" is it replaces the Nil constructor of the list with the z argument, and it replaces the Cons constructor with the given function, f. If we just supply Nil for z and Cons for f, then we get back the input list.

```
foldRight(Cons(1, Cons(2, Cons(3, Nil))), Nil:List[Int])(Cons(_,_))
Cons(1, foldRight(Cons(2, Cons(3, Nil)), Nil:List[Int])(Cons(_,_)))
Cons(1, Cons(2, foldRight(Cons(3, Nil), Nil:List[Int])(Cons(_,_))))
Cons(1, Cons(2, Cons(3, foldRight(Nil, Nil:List[Int])(Cons(_,_)))))
Cons(1, Cons(2, Cons(3, Nil)))
```

Exercise 3.09

```
def length[A](l: List[A]): Int =
  foldRight(l, 0)((_,acc) => acc + 1)
```

Exercise 3.10

It's common practice to annotate functions you expect to be tail-recursive with the tailrec annotation. If the function is not tail-recursive, it will yield a compile error, rather than silently compiling the code and resulting in greater stack space usage at runtime.

```
@annotation.tailrec
def foldLeft[A,B](l: List[A], z: B)(f: (B, A) => B): B = l match {
  case Nil => z
  case Cons(h,t) => foldLeft(t, f(z,h))(f)
}
```

Exercise 3.11

```
def sum3(l: List[Int]) = foldLeft(l, 0)(_ + _)
def product3(l: List[Double]) = foldLeft(l, 1.0)(_ * _)

def length2[A](l: List[A]): Int = foldLeft(l, 0)((acc,h) => acc + 1)
```

Exercise 3.12

```
def reverse[A](l: List[A]): List[A] =
  foldLeft(l, List[A]())((acc,h) => Cons(h,acc))
```

Exercise 3.13

The implementation of `foldRight` in terms of `reverse` and `foldLeft` is a common trick for avoiding stack overflows when implementing a strict `foldRight` function as we've done in this chapter. (We'll revisit this in a later chapter, when we discuss laziness).

The other implementations build up a chain of functions which, when called, results in the operations being performed with the correct associativity. We are calling `foldRight` with the B type being instantiated to `B => B`, then calling the built up function with the z argument. Try expanding the definitions by substituting equals for equals using a simple example, like `foldLeft(List(1,2,3), 0)(_ + _)` if this isn't clear. Note these implementations are more of theoretical interest - they aren't stack-safe and won't work for large lists.

```
def foldRightViaFoldLeft[A,B](l: List[A], z: B)(f: (A,B) => B): B =
  foldLeft(reverse(l), z)((b,a) => f(a,b))

def foldRightViaFoldLeft_1[A,B](l: List[A], z: B)(f: (A,B) => B): B =
  foldLeft(l, (b:B) => b)((g,a) => b => g(f(a,b)))(z)

def foldLeftViaFoldRight[A,B](l: List[A], z: B)(f: (B,A) => B): B =
  foldRight(l, (b:B) => b)((a,g) => b => g(f(b,a)))(z)
```

Exercise 3.14

`append` simply replaces the `Nil` constructor of the first list with the second list, which is exactly the operation performed by `foldRight`.

```
def appendViaFoldRight[A](l: List[A], r: List[A]): List[A] =
  foldRight(l, r)(Cons(_,_))
```

Exercise 3.15

Since `append` takes time proportional to its first argument, and this first argument never grows because of the right-associativity of `foldRight`, this function is linear in the total length of all lists. You may want to try tracing the execution of the implementation on paper to convince yourself that this works.

Note that we're simply referencing the `append` function, without writing something like `(x,y) => append(x,y)` or `append(_,_)`. In Scala there is a rather arbitrary distinction between functions defined as *methods*, which are introduced with the `def` keyword, and function values, which are the first-class objects we can pass to other functions, put in collections, and so on. This is a case where Scala lets us pretend the distinction doesn't exist. In other cases, you'll be forced to write `append` _ (to convert a `def` to a function value) or even `(x: List[A], y: List[A]) => append(x,y)` if the function is polymorphic and the type arguments aren't known.

```
def concat[A](l: List[List[A]]): List[A] =
  foldRight(l, Nil:List[A])(append)
```

Exercise 3.16

```
def add1(l: List[Int]): List[Int] =
  foldRight(l, Nil:List[Int])((h,t) => Cons(h+1,t))
```

Exercise 3.17

```
def doubleToString(l: List[Double]): List[String] =
  foldRight(l, Nil:List[String])((h,t) => Cons(h.toString,t))
```

Exercise 3.18

A natural solution is using `foldRight`, but our implementation of `foldRight` is not stack-safe. We can use `foldRightViaFoldLeft` to avoid the stack overflow (variation 1), but more commonly, with our current implementation of `List`, `map` will just be implemented using local mutation (variation 2). Again, note that the mutation isn't observable outside the function, since we're only mutating a buffer that we've allocated.

```
def map[A,B](l: List[A])(f: A => B): List[B] =
  foldRight(l, Nil:List[B])((h,t) => Cons(f(h),t))

def map_1[A,B](l: List[A])(f: A => B): List[B] =
  foldRightViaFoldLeft(l, Nil:List[B])((h,t) => Cons(f(h),t))

def map_2[A,B](l: List[A])(f: A => B): List[B] = {
  val buf = new collection.mutable.ListBuffer[B]
  def go(l: List[A]): Unit = l match {
    case Nil => ()
    case Cons(h,t) => buf += f(h); go(t)
  }
  go(l)
  List(buf.toList: _*)
  // converting from the standard Scala list to the list we've defined here
}
```

Exercise 3.19

```
/*
The discussion about `map` also applies here.
*/
def filter[A](l: List[A])(f: A => Boolean): List[A] =
  foldRight(l, Nil:List[A])((h,t) => if (f(h)) Cons(h,t) else t)

def filter_1[A](l: List[A])(f: A => Boolean): List[A] =
  foldRightViaFoldLeft(l, Nil:List[A])((h,t) => if (f(h)) Cons(h,t) else t)

def filter_2[A](l: List[A])(f: A => Boolean): List[A] = {
  val buf = new collection.mutable.ListBuffer[A]
  def go(l: List[A]): Unit = l match {
    case Nil => ()
    case Cons(h,t) => if (f(h)) buf += h; go(t)
  }
  go(l)
  List(buf.toList: _*)
  // converting from the standard Scala list to the list we've defined here
}
```

Exercise 3.20

```
/*
This could also be implemented directly using `foldRight`.
*/
def flatMap[A,B](l: List[A])(f: A => List[B]): List[B] =
  concat(map(l)(f))
```

Exercise 3.21

```
def filterViaFlatMap[A](l: List[A])(f: A => Boolean): List[A] =
  flatMap(l)(a => if (f(a)) List(a) else Nil)
```

Exercise 3.22

To match on multiple values, we can put the values into a pair and match on the pair, as shown next, and the same syntax extends to matching on N values (see sidebar "Pairs and tuples in Scala" for more about pair and tuple objects). You can also (somewhat less conveniently, but a bit more efficiently) nest pattern matches: on the right hand side of the =>, simply begin another match expression. The inner match will have access to all the variables introduced in the outer match.

The discussion about stack usage from the explanation of map also applies here.

```
def addPairwise(a: List[Int], b: List[Int]): List[Int] = (a,b) match {
  case (Nil, _) => Nil
  case (_, Nil) => Nil
  case (Cons(h1,t1), Cons(h2,t2)) => Cons(h1+h2, addPairwise(t1,t2))
}
```

Exercise 3.23

This function is usually called `zipWith`. The discussion about stack usage from the explanation of `map` also applies here. By putting the `f` in the second argument list, Scala can infer its type from the previous argument list.

```
def zipWith[A,B,C](a: List[A], b: List[B])(f: (A,B) => C): List[C] =
  (a,b) match {
    case (Nil, _) => Nil
    case (_, Nil) => Nil
    case (Cons(h1,t1), Cons(h2,t2)) => Cons(f(h1,h2), zipWith(t1,t2)(f))
  }
```

Exercise 3.24

It's good to specify some properties about these functions. For example, do you expect these expressions to be true?

```
(xs append ys) startsWith xs
```

```
xs startsWith Nil
```

```
(xs append ys append zs) hasSubsequence ys
```

```
xs hasSubsequence Nil
```

Here is one solution where those properties do in fact hold. There's nothing particularly bad about this implementation, except that it's somewhat monolithic and easy to get wrong. Where possible, we prefer to assemble functions like this using combinations of other functions. It makes the code more obviously correct and easier to read and understand. Notice that in this implementation we need special purpose logic to break out of our loops early. In Chapter 5 we'll discuss ways of composing functions like this from simpler components, without giving up the efficiency of having the resulting functions work in one pass over the data.

```
@annotation.tailrec
def startsWith[A](l: List[A], prefix: List[A]): Boolean = (l,prefix) match {
  case (_,Nil) => true
  case (Cons(h,t),Cons(h2,t2)) if h == h2 => startsWith(t, t2)
  case _ => false
}
@annotation.tailrec
def hasSubsequence[A](sup: List[A], sub: List[A]): Boolean = sup match {
  case Nil => sub == Nil
  case _ => startsWith(sup, sub)
  case Cons(h,t) => hasSubsequence(t, sub)
}
```

Exercise 3.25

```
def size[A](t: Tree[A]): Int = t match {
  case Leaf(_) => 1
  case Branch(l,r) => 1 + size(l) + size(r)
}
```

Exercise 3.26

We're using the method max that exists on all Int values rather than an explicit if expression.

Note how similar the implementation is to size. We'll abstract out the common pattern in a later exercise.

```
def maximum(t: Tree[Int]): Int = t match {
  case Leaf(n) => n
  case Branch(l,r) => maximum(l) max maximum(r)
}
```

Exercise 3.27

Again, note how similar the implementation is to size and maximum.

```
def depth[A](t: Tree[A]): Int = t match {
  case Leaf(_) => 0
  case Branch(l,r) => 1 + (depth(l) max depth(r))
}
```

Exercise 3.28

```
def map[A,B](t: Tree[A])(f: A => B): Tree[B] = t match {
  case Leaf(a) => Leaf(f(a))
  case Branch(l,r) => Branch(map(l)(f), map(r)(f))
}
```

Exercise 3.29

```
def mapViaFold[A,B](t: Tree[A])(f: A => B): Tree[B] =
  fold(t)(a => Leaf(f(a)): Tree[B])(Branch(_,_))
```

Like `foldRight` for lists, `fold` receives a "handler" for each of the data constructors of the type, and recursively accumulates some value using these handlers. As with `foldRight`, `fold(t)(Leaf(_))(Branch(_,_))` == t, and we can use this function to implement just about any recursive function that would otherwise be defined by pattern matching.

```
def fold[A,B](t: Tree[A])(f: A => B)(g: (B,B) => B): B = t match {
  case Leaf(a) => f(a)
  case Branch(l,r) => g(fold(l)(f)(g), fold(r)(f)(g))
}

def sizeViaFold[A](t: Tree[A]): Int =
  fold(t)(a => 1)(1 + _ + _)

def maximumViaFold(t: Tree[Int]): Int =
  fold(t)(a => a)(_ max _)

def depthViaFold[A](t: Tree[A]): Int =
  fold(t)(a => 0)((d1,d2) => 1 + (d1 max d2))
```

Note the type annotation required on the expression `Leaf(f(a))`. Without this annotation, we get an error like this:

```
type mismatch;
  found   : fpinscala.datastructures.Branch[B]
  required: fpinscala.datastructures.Leaf[B]
    fold(t)(a => Leaf(f(a)))(Branch(_,_))
                                ^
```

This error is an unfortunate consequence of Scala using subtyping to encode algebraic data types. Without the annotation, the result type of the fold gets inferred as `Leaf[B]` and it is then expected that the second argument to `fold` will return `Leaf[B]`, which it doesn't (it returns `Branch[B]`). Really, we'd prefer Scala to infer `Tree[B]` as the result type in both cases. When working with algebraic data types in Scala, it's somewhat common to define helper functions that simply call the corresponding data constructors but give the less specific result type:

```
def leaf[A](a: A): Tree[A] = Leaf(a)
def branch[A](l: Tree[A], r: Tree[A]): Tree[A] = Branch(l, r)
```

Answers to exercises for chapter 4

Exercise 4.01

```
def map[B](f: A => B): Option[B] = this match {
  case None => None
  case Some(a) => Some(f(a))
}

def getOrElse[B>:A](default: => B): B = this match {
  case None => default
  case Some(a) => a
}

def flatMap[B](f: A => Option[B]): Option[B] =
  map(f) getOrElse None

/*
Of course, we can also implement `flatMap` with explicit pattern matching.
*/
def flatMap_1[B](f: A => Option[B]): Option[B] = this match {
  case None => None
  case Some(a) => f(a)
}

def orElse[B>:A](ob: => Option[B]): Option[B] =
  this map (Some(_)) getOrElse ob

/*
Again, we can implement this with explicit pattern matching.
*/
def orElse_1[B>:A](ob: => Option[B]): Option[B] = this match {
  case None => ob
  case _ => this
}

/*
This can also be defined in terms of `flatMap`.
*/
def filter_1(f: A => Boolean): Option[A] =
  flatMap(a => if (f(a)) Some(a) else None)
```

```
/* Or via explicit pattern matching. */
def filter(f: A => Boolean): Option[A] = this match {
  case Some(a) if f(a) => this
  case _ => None
}
```

Exercise 4.02

```
def variance(xs: Seq[Double]): Option[Double] =
  mean(xs) flatMap (m => mean(xs.map(x => math.pow(x - m, 2))))
```

Exercise 4.03

A bit later in the chapter we'll learn nicer syntax for writing functions like this.

```
def map2[A,B,C](a: Option[A], b: Option[B])(f: (A, B) => C): Option[C] =
  a flatMap (aa => b map (bb => f(aa, bb)))
```

Exercise 4.04

Here's an explicit recursive version:

```
def sequence[A](a: List[Option[A]]): Option[List[A]] =
  a match {
    case Nil => Some(Nil)
    case h :: t => h flatMap (hh => sequence(t) map (hh :: _))
  }
```

It can also be implemented using foldRight and map2. The type annotation on foldRight is needed here; otherwise Scala wrongly infers the result type of the fold as Some[Nil.type] and reports a type error (try it!). This is an unfortunate consequence of Scala using subtyping to encode algebraic data types.

```
def sequence_1[A](a: List[Option[A]]): Option[List[A]] =
  a.foldRight[Option[List[A]]](Some(Nil))((x,y) => map2(x,y)(_ :: _))
```

Exercise 4.05

```
def traverse[A, B](a: List[A])(f: A => Option[B]): Option[List[B]] =
  a match {
    case Nil => Some(Nil)
    case h::t => map2(f(h), traverse(t)(f))(_ :: _)
  }


def traverse_1[A, B](a: List[A])(f: A => Option[B]): Option[List[B]] =
  a.foldRight[Option[List[B]]](Some(Nil))((h,t) => map2(f(h),t)(_ :: _))

def sequenceViaTraverse[A](a: List[Option[A]]): Option[List[A]] =
  traverse(a)(x => x)
```

Exercise 4.06

```
def map[B](f: A => B): Either[E, B] =
  this match {
    case Right(a) => Right(f(a))
    case Left(e) => Left(e)
  }


def flatMap[EE >: E, B](f: A => Either[EE, B]): Either[EE, B] =
  this match {
    case Left(e) => Left(e)
    case Right(a) => f(a)
  }
def orElse[EE >: E, AA >: A](b: => Either[EE, AA]): Either[EE, AA] =
  this match {
    case Left(_) => b
    case Right(a) => Right(a)
  }
def map2[EE >: E, B, C](b: Either[EE, B])(f: (A, B) => C):
  Either[EE, C] = for { a <- this; b1 <- b } yield f(a,b1)
```

Exercise 4.07

```
def traverse[E,A,B](es: List[A])(f: A => Either[E, B]): Either[E, List[B]] =
  es match {
    case Nil => Right(Nil)
    case h::t => (f(h) map2 traverse(t)(f))(_ :: _)
  }

def traverse_1[E,A,B](es: List[A])(f: A => Either[E, B]): Either[E, List[B]] =
  es.foldRight[Either[E,List[B]]](Right(Nil))((a, b) => f(a).map2(b)(_ :: _))

def sequence[E,A](es: List[Either[E,A]]): Either[E,List[A]] =
  traverse(es)(x => x)
```

Exercise 4.08

There are a number of variations on Option and Either. If we want to accumulate multiple errors, a simple approach is a new data type that lets us keep a list of errors in the data constructor that represents failures:

```
trait Partial[+A,+B]
case class Errors[+A](get: Seq[A]) extends Partial[A,Nothing]
case class Success[+B](get: B) extends Partial[Nothing,B]
```

There is a type very similar to this called Validation in the Scalaz library. You can implement map, map2, sequence, and so on for this type in such a way that errors are accumulated when possible (flatMap is unable to accumulate errors–can you see why?). This idea can even be generalized further–we don't need to accumulate failing values into a list; we can accumulate values using any user-supplied binary function.

It's also possible to use Either[List[E],_] directly to accumulate errors, using different implementations of helper functions like map2 and sequence.

Answers to exercises for chapter 5

Exercise 5.01

```
// The natural recursive solution
def toListRecursive: List[A] = this match {
  case Cons(h,t) => h() :: t().toListRecursive
  case _ => List()
}
```

The above solution will stack overflow for large streams, since it's not tail-recursive. Here is a tail-recursive implementation. At each step we cons onto the front of the acc list, which will result in the reverse of the stream. Then at the end we reverse the result to get the correct order again.

```
def toList: List[A] = {
  @annotation.tailrec
  def go(s: Stream[A], acc: List[A]): List[A] = s match {
    case Cons(h,t) => go(t(), h() :: acc)
    case _ => acc
  }
  go(this, List()).reverse
}
```

In order to avoid the reverse at the end, we could write it using a mutable list buffer and an explicit loop instead. Note that the mutable list buffer never escapes our toList method, so this function is still *pure*.

```
def toListFast: List[A] = {
  val buf = new collection.mutable.ListBuffer[A]
  @annotation.tailrec
  def go(s: Stream[A]): List[A] = s match {
    case Cons(h,t) =>
      buf += h()
      go(t())
    case _ => buf.toList
  }
  go(this)
}
```

Exercise 5.02

take first checks if n==0. In that case we need not look at the stream at all.

```
def take(n: Int): Stream[A] = this match {
  case Cons(h, t) if n > 1 => cons(h(), t().take(n - 1))
  case Cons(h, _) if n == 1 => cons(h(), empty)
  case _ => empty
}
```

Unlike take, drop is not incremental. That is, it doesn't generate the answer lazily. It must traverse the first n elements of the stream eagerly.

```
@annotation.tailrec
final def drop(n: Int): Stream[A] = this match {
  case Cons(_, t) if n > 0 => t().drop(n - 1)
  case _ => this
}
```

Exercise 5.03

It's a common Scala style to write method calls without . notation, as in t() takeWhile f.

```
def takeWhile(f: A => Boolean): Stream[A] = this match {
  case Cons(h,t) if f(h()) => cons(h(), t() takeWhile f)
  case _ => empty
}
```

Exercise 5.04

Since && is non-strict in its second argument, this terminates the traversal as soon as a nonmatching element is found.

```
def forAll(f: A => Boolean): Boolean =
  foldRight(true)((a,b) => f(a) && b)
```

Exercise 5.05

```
def takeWhile_1(f: A => Boolean): Stream[A] =
  foldRight(empty[A])((h,t) =>
    if (f(h)) cons(h,t)
    else      empty)
```

Exercise 5.06

```
def headOption: Option[A] =
  foldRight(None: Option[A])((h,_) => Some(h))
```

Exercise 5.07

```
def map[B](f: A => B): Stream[B] =
  foldRight(empty[B])((h,t) => cons(f(h), t))

def filter(f: A => Boolean): Stream[A] =
  foldRight(empty[A])((h,t) =>
    if (f(h)) cons(h, t)
    else t)

def append[B>:A](s: => Stream[B]): Stream[B] =
  foldRight(s)((h,t) => cons(h,t))

def flatMap[B](f: A => Stream[B]): Stream[B] =
  foldRight(empty[B])((h,t) => f(h) append t)
```

Exercise 5.08

```
// This is more efficient than `cons(a, constant(a))` since it's just
// one object referencing itself.
def constant[A](a: A): Stream[A] = {
  lazy val tail: Stream[A] = Cons(() => a, () => tail)
  tail
}
```

Exercise 5.09

```
def from(n: Int): Stream[Int] =
  cons(n, from(n+1))
```

Exercise 5.10

```
val fibs = {
  def go(f0: Int, f1: Int): Stream[Int] =
    cons(f0, go(f1, f0+f1))
  go(0, 1)
}
```

Exercise 5.11

```scala
def unfold[A, S](z: S)(f: S => Option[(A, S)]): Stream[A] =
  f(z) match {
    case Some((h,s)) => cons(h, unfold(s)(f))
    case None => empty
  }
```

Exercise 5.12

Scala provides shorter syntax when the first action of a function literal is to match on an expression. The function passed to `unfold` in `fibsViaUnfold` is equivalent to `p => p match { case (f0,f1) => ... }`, but we avoid having to choose a name for `p`, only to pattern match on it.

```scala
val fibsViaUnfold =
  unfold((0,1)) { case (f0,f1) => Some((f0,(f1,f0+f1))) }

def fromViaUnfold(n: Int) =
  unfold(n)(n => Some((n,n+1)))

def constantViaUnfold[A](a: A) =
  unfold(a)(_ => Some((a,a)))

// could also of course be implemented as constant(1)
val onesViaUnfold = unfold(1)(_ => Some((1,1)))
```

Exercise 5.13

```scala
def mapViaUnfold[B](f: A => B): Stream[B] =
  unfold(this) {
    case Cons(h,t) => Some((f(h()), t()))
    case _ => None
  }

def takeViaUnfold(n: Int): Stream[A] =
  unfold((this,n)) {
    case (Cons(h,t), 1) => Some((h(), (empty, 0)))
    case (Cons(h,t), n) if n > 1 => Some((h(), (t(), n-1)))
    case _ => None
  }

def takeWhileViaUnfold(f: A => Boolean): Stream[A] =
  unfold(this) {
    case Cons(h,t) if f(h()) => Some((h(), t()))
    case _ => None
  }
```

```
def zipWith[B,C](s2: Stream[B])(f: (A,B) => C): Stream[C] =
  unfold((this, s2)) {
    case (Cons(h1,t1), Cons(h2,t2)) =>
      Some((f(h1(), h2()), (t1(), t2())))
    case _ => None
  }

// special case of `zip`
def zip[B](s2: Stream[B]): Stream[(A,B)] =
  zipWith(s2)((_,_))


def zipAll[B](s2: Stream[B]): Stream[(Option[A],Option[B])] =
  zipWithAll(s2)((_,_))

def zipWithAll[B, C](s2: Stream[B])(f: (Option[A], Option[B]) => C): Stream[C] =
  Stream.unfold((this, s2)) {
    case (Empty, Empty) => None
    case (Cons(h, t), Empty) => Some(f(Some(h()), Option.empty[B]) -> (t(), empty[B]))
    case (Empty, Cons(h, t)) => Some(f(Option.empty[A], Some(h())) -> (empty[A] -> t()))
    case (Cons(h1, t1), Cons(h2, t2)) => Some(f(Some(h1()), Some(h2())) -> (t1() -> t2()))
  }
```

Exercise 5.14

s startsWith s2 when corresponding elements of s and s2 are all equal, until the point that s2
is exhausted. If s is exhausted first, or we find an element that doesn't match, we terminate early.
Using non-strictness, we can compose these three separate logical steps–the zipping, the termination
when the second stream is exhausted, and the termination if a nonmatching element is found or the
first stream is exhausted.

```
def startsWith[A](s: Stream[A]): Boolean =
  zipAll(s).takeWhile(!_._2.isEmpty) forAll {
    case (h,h2) => h == h2
  }
```

Exercise 5.15

The last element of tails is always the empty Stream, so we handle this as a special case, by
appending it to the output.

```
def tails: Stream[Stream[A]] =
  unfold(this) {
    case Empty => None
    case s => Some((s, s drop 1))
  } append Stream(empty)
```

Exercise 5.16

The function can't be implemented using `unfold`, since `unfold` generates elements of the `Stream` from left to right. It can be implemented using `foldRight` though.

The implementation is just a `foldRight` that keeps the accumulated value and the stream of intermediate results, which we `cons` onto during each iteration. When writing folds, it's common to have more state in the fold than is needed to compute the result. Here, we simply extract the accumulated list once finished.

```
def scanRight[B](z: B)(f: (A, => B) => B): Stream[B] =
  foldRight((z, Stream(z)))((a, p0) => {
    // p0 is passed by-name and used in by-name args in f and cons.
    // So use lazy val to ensure only one evaluation...
    lazy val p1 = p0
    val b2 = f(a, p1._1)
    (b2, cons(b2, p1._2))
  })._2
```

Answers to exercises for chapter 6

Exercise 6.01

We need to be quite careful not to skew the generator. Since `Int.Minvalue` is 1 smaller than `-(Int.MaxValue)`, it suffices to increment the negative numbers by 1 and make them positive. This maps Int.MinValue to Int.MaxValue and -1 to 0.

```
def nonNegativeInt(rng: RNG): (Int, RNG) = {
  val (i, r) = rng.nextInt
  (if (i < 0) -(i + 1) else i, r)
}
```

Exercise 6.02

We generate an integer >= 0 and divide it by one higher than the maximum. This is just one possible solution.

```
def double(rng: RNG): (Double, RNG) = {
  val (i, r) = nonNegativeInt(rng)
  (i / (Int.MaxValue.toDouble + 1), r)
}
```

Exercise 6.03

```
def intDouble(rng: RNG): ((Int, Double), RNG) = {
  val (i, r1) = rng.nextInt
  val (d, r2) = double(r1)
  ((i, d), r2)
}
```

```
def doubleInt(rng: RNG): ((Double, Int), RNG) = {
  val ((i, d), r) = intDouble(rng)
  ((d, i), r)
}
```

```
def double3(rng: RNG): ((Double, Double, Double), RNG) = {
  val (d1, r1) = double(rng)
  val (d2, r2) = double(r1)
  val (d3, r3) = double(r2)
  ((d1, d2, d3), r3)
}
```

There is something terribly repetitive about passing the RNG along every time. What could we do to eliminate some of this duplication of effort?

Exercise 6.04

```
// A simple recursive solution
def ints(count: Int)(rng: RNG): (List[Int], RNG) =
  if (count == 0)
    (List(), rng)
  else {
    val (x, r1)  = rng.nextInt
    val (xs, r2) = ints(count - 1)(r1)
    (x :: xs, r2)
  }
```

```
// A tail-recursive solution
def ints2(count: Int)(rng: RNG): (List[Int], RNG) = {
  def go(count: Int, r: RNG, xs: List[Int]): (List[Int], RNG) =
    if (count == 0)
```

```
      (xs, r)
    else {
      val (x, r2) = r.nextInt
      go(count - 1, r2, x :: xs)
    }
  go(count, rng, List())
}
```

Exercise 6.05

```
val _double: Rand[Double] =
  map(nonNegativeInt)(_ / (Int.MaxValue.toDouble + 1))
```

Exercise 6.06

This implementation of map2 passes the initial RNG to the first argument and the resulting RNG to the second argument. It's not necessarily wrong to do this the other way around, since the results are random anyway. We could even pass the initial RNG to both f and g, but that might have unexpected results. E.g. if both arguments are RNG.int then we would always get two of the same Int in the result. When implementing functions like this, it's important to consider how we would test them for correctness.

```
def map2[A,B,C](ra: Rand[A], rb: Rand[B])(f: (A, B) => C): Rand[C] =
  rng => {
    val (a, r1) = ra(rng)
    val (b, r2) = rb(r1)
    (f(a, b), r2)
  }
```

Exercise 6.07

In sequence, the base case of the fold is a unit action that returns the empty list. At each step in the fold, we accumulate in acc and f is the current element in the list. map2(f, acc)(_ :: _) results in a value of type Rand[List[A]] We map over that to prepend (cons) the element onto the accumulated list.

We are using foldRight. If we used foldLeft then the values in the resulting list would appear in reverse order. It would be arguably better to use foldLeft followed by reverse. What do you think?

```
def sequence[A](fs: List[Rand[A]]): Rand[List[A]] =
  fs.foldRight(unit(List[A]()))((f, acc) => map2(f, acc)(_ :: _))
```

It's interesting that we never actually need to talk about the RNG value in sequence. This is a strong hint that we could make this function polymorphic in that type.

```
def _ints(count: Int): Rand[List[Int]] =
  sequence(List.fill(count)(int))
```

Exercise 6.08

```
def flatMap[A,B](f: Rand[A])(g: A => Rand[B]): Rand[B] =
  rng => {
    val (a, r1) = f(rng)
    g(a)(r1) // We pass the new state along
  }

def nonNegativeLessThan(n: Int): Rand[Int] = {
  flatMap(nonNegativeInt) { i =>
    val mod = i % n
    if (i + (n-1) - mod >= 0) unit(mod) else nonNegativeLessThan(n)
  }
}
```

Exercise 6.09

```
def _map[A,B](s: Rand[A])(f: A => B): Rand[B] =
  flatMap(s)(a => unit(f(a)))

def _map2[A,B,C](ra: Rand[A], rb: Rand[B])(f: (A, B) => C): Rand[C] =
  flatMap(ra)(a => map(rb)(b => f(a, b)))
```

Exercise 6.10

```
case class State[S, +A](run: S => (A, S)) {
  def map[B](f: A => B): State[S, B] =
    flatMap(a => unit(f(a)))
  def map2[B,C](sb: State[S, B])(f: (A, B) => C): State[S, C] =
    flatMap(a => sb.map(b => f(a, b)))
  def flatMap[B](f: A => State[S, B]): State[S, B] = State(s => {
    val (a, s1) = run(s)
    f(a).run(s1)
  })
}

object State {

  def unit[S, A](a: A): State[S, A] =
    State(s => (a, s))
```

```
  // The idiomatic solution is expressed via foldRight
  def sequenceViaFoldRight[S,A](sas: List[State[S, A]]): State[S, List[A]] =
    sas.foldRight(unit[S, List[A]](List()))((f, acc) => f.map2(acc)(_ :: _))


  // This implementation uses a loop internally and is the same recursion
  // pattern as a left fold. It is quite common with left folds to build
  // up a list in reverse order, then reverse it at the end.
  // (We could also use a collection.mutable.ListBuffer internally.)
  def sequence[S, A](sas: List[State[S, A]]): State[S, List[A]] = {
    def go(s: S, actions: List[State[S,A]], acc: List[A]): (List[A],S) =
      actions match {
        case Nil => (acc.reverse,s)
        case h :: t => h.run(s) match { case (a,s2) => go(s2, t, a :: acc) }
      }
    State((s: S) => go(s,sas,List()))
  }


  // We can also write the loop using a left fold. This is tail recursive like
  // the previous solution, but it reverses the list _before_ folding it instead
  // of after. You might think that this is slower than the `foldRight` solution
  // since it walks over the list twice, but it's actually faster! The
  // `foldRight` solution technically has to also walk the list twice, since it
  // has to unravel the call stack, not being tail recursive. And the call stack
  // will be as tall as the list is long.
  def sequenceViaFoldLeft[S,A](l: List[State[S, A]]): State[S, List[A]] =
    l.reverse.foldLeft(unit[S, List[A]](List())) {
      (acc, f) => f.map2(acc)( _ :: _ )
    }


  def modify[S](f: S => S): State[S, Unit] = for {
    s <- get // Gets the current state and assigns it to `s`.
    _ <- set(f(s)) // Sets the new state to `f` applied to `s`.
  } yield ()

  def get[S]: State[S, S] = State(s => (s, s))

  def set[S](s: S): State[S, Unit] = State(_ => ((), s))
}
```

Exercise 6.11

```scala
sealed trait Input
case object Coin extends Input
case object Turn extends Input

case class Machine(locked: Boolean, candies: Int, coins: Int)

object Candy {
  def simulateMachine(inputs: List[Input]): State[Machine, (Int, Int)] = for {
    _ <- sequence(inputs.map(i => modify((s: Machine) => (i, s) match {
      case (_, Machine(_, 0, _)) => s
      case (Coin, Machine(false, _, _)) => s
      case (Turn, Machine(true, _, _)) => s
      case (Coin, Machine(true, candy, coin)) =>
        Machine(false, candy, coin + 1)
      case (Turn, Machine(false, candy, coin)) =>
        Machine(true, candy - 1, coin)
    })))
    s <- get
  } yield (s.coins, s.candies)
}
```

Answers to exercises for chapter 7

Exercise 7.01

```scala
/* def map2[A,B,C](a: Par[A], b: Par[B])(f: (A,B) => C): Par[C] */
```

Exercise 7.02

Keep reading - we choose a representation for Par later in the chapter.

Exercise 7.03

```
/* This version respects timeouts. See `Map2Future` below. */
def map2[A,B,C](a: Par[A], b: Par[B])(f: (A,B) => C): Par[C] =
  es => {
    val (af, bf) = (a(es), b(es))
    Map2Future(af, bf, f)
  }


/*
Note: this implementation will not prevent repeated evaluation if multiple
threads call `get` in parallel. We could prevent this using synchronization,
but it isn't needed for our purposes here (also, repeated evaluation of pure
values won't affect results).
*/
case class Map2Future[A,B,C](a: Future[A], b: Future[B],
                             f: (A,B) => C) extends Future[C] {
  @volatile var cache: Option[C] = None
  def isDone = cache.isDefined
  def isCancelled = a.isCancelled || b.isCancelled
  def cancel(evenIfRunning: Boolean) =
    a.cancel(evenIfRunning) || b.cancel(evenIfRunning)
  def get = compute(Long.MaxValue)
  def get(timeout: Long, units: TimeUnit): C =
    compute(TimeUnit.MILLISECONDS.convert(timeout, units))

  private def compute(timeoutMs: Long): C = cache match {
    case Some(c) => c
    case None =>
      val start = System.currentTimeMillis
      val ar = a.get(timeoutMs, TimeUnit.MILLISECONDS)
      val stop = System.currentTimeMillis; val at = stop-start
      val br = b.get(timeoutMs - at, TimeUnit.MILLISECONDS)
      val ret = f(ar, br)
      cache = Some(ret)
      ret
  }
}
```

Exercise 7.04

```
def asyncF[A,B](f: A => B): A => Par[B] =
  a => lazyUnit(f(a))
```

Exercise 7.05

```
def sequence_simple[A](l: List[Par[A]]): Par[List[A]] =
  l.foldRight[Par[List[A]]](unit(List()))((h,t) => map2(h,t)(_ :: _))
```

```scala
// This implementation forks the recursive step off to a new logical thread,
// making it effectively tail-recursive. However, we are constructing
// a right-nested parallel program, and we can get better performance by
// dividing the list in half, and running both halves in parallel.
// See `sequenceBalanced` below.
def sequenceRight[A](as: List[Par[A]]): Par[List[A]] =
  as match {
    case Nil => unit(Nil)
    case h :: t => map2(h, fork(sequence(t)))(_ :: _)
  }
```

```scala
// We define `sequenceBalanced` using `IndexedSeq`, which provides an
// efficient function for splitting the sequence in half.
def sequenceBalanced[A](as: IndexedSeq[Par[A]]): Par[IndexedSeq[A]] = fork {
  if (as.isEmpty) unit(Vector())
  else if (as.length == 1) map(as.head)(a => Vector(a))
  else {
    val (l,r) = as.splitAt(as.length/2)
    map2(sequenceBalanced(l), sequenceBalanced(r))(_ ++ _)
  }
}
```

```
def sequence[A](as: List[Par[A]]): Par[List[A]] =
  map(sequenceBalanced(as.toIndexedSeq))(_.toList)
```

Exercise 7.06

```scala
def parFilter[A](l: List[A])(f: A => Boolean): Par[List[A]] = {
  val pars: List[Par[List[A]]] =
    l map (asyncF((a: A) => if (f(a)) List(a) else List()))
  // flatten is a convenience method on `List` for concatenating a list of lists
  map(sequence(pars))(_.flatten)
}
```

Exercise 7.07

See https://github.com/quchen/articles/blob/master/second_functor_law.md

Also https://gist.github.com/pchiusano/444de1f222f1ceb09596

Exercise 7.08

Keep reading. The issue is explained in the next paragraph.

Exercise 7.09

For a thread pool of size 2, `fork(fork(fork(x)))` will deadlock, and so on. Another, perhaps more interesting example is `fork(map2(fork(x), fork(y)))`. In this case, the outer task is submitted first and occupies a thread waiting for both `fork(x)` and `fork(y)`. The `fork(x)` and `fork(y)` tasks are submitted and run in parallel, except that only one thread is available, resulting in deadlock.

Exercise 7.10

We give a fully fleshed-out solution in the `Task` data type in the code for Chapter 13.

Exercise 7.11

```scala
def choiceN[A](n: Par[Int])(choices: List[Par[A]]): Par[A] =
  es => {
    val ind = run(es)(n).get // Full source files
    run(es)(choices(ind))
  }


def choiceViaChoiceN[A](a: Par[Boolean])(ifTrue: Par[A], ifFalse: Par[A]): Par[A] =
  choiceN(map(a)(b => if (b) 0 else 1))(List(ifTrue, ifFalse))
```

Exercise 7.12

```scala
def choiceMap[K,V](key: Par[K])(choices: Map[K,Par[V]]): Par[V] =
  es => {
    val k = run(es)(key).get
    run(es)(choices(k))
  }
```

Exercise 7.13

```scala
def chooser[A,B](p: Par[A])(choices: A => Par[B]): Par[B] =
  es => {
    val k = run(es)(p).get
    run(es)(choices(k))
  }

/* `chooser` is usually called `flatMap` or `bind`. */
def flatMap[A,B](p: Par[A])(choices: A => Par[B]): Par[B] =
  es => {
    val k = run(es)(p).get
    run(es)(choices(k))
```

```
  }

def choiceViaFlatMap[A](p: Par[Boolean])(f: Par[A], t: Par[A]): Par[A] =
  flatMap(p)(b => if (b) t else f)

def choiceNViaFlatMap[A](p: Par[Int])(choices: List[Par[A]]): Par[A] =
  flatMap(p)(i => choices(i))
```

Exercise 7.14

```
// see nonblocking implementation in `Nonblocking.scala`
def join[A](a: Par[Par[A]]): Par[A] =
  es => run(es)(run(es)(a).get())

def joinViaFlatMap[A](a: Par[Par[A]]): Par[A] =
  flatMap(a)(x => x)

def flatMapViaJoin[A,B](p: Par[A])(f: A => Par[B]): Par[B] =
  join(map(p)(f))
```

Exercise 7.15

```
def flatMap[B](f: A => Par[B]): Par[B] =
  Par.flatMap(p)(f)

def map[B](f: A => B): Par[B] =
  Par.map(p)(f)

def map2[B,C](p2: Par[B])(f: (A,B) => C): Par[C] =
  Par.map2(p,p2)(f)

def zip[B](p2: Par[B]): Par[(A,B)] =
  p.map2(p2)((_,_))
```

Exercise 7.16

```
def flatMap[B](f: A => Par[B]): Par[B] =
  Par.flatMap(p)(f)

def map[B](f: A => B): Par[B] =
  Par.map(p)(f)

def map2[B,C](p2: Par[B])(f: (A,B) => C): Par[C] =
  Par.map2(p,p2)(f)

def zip[B](p2: Par[B]): Par[(A,B)] =
  p.map2(p2)((_,_))
```

Exercise 7.17

This implementation is not safe for execution on bounded thread pools, and it also does not preserve timeouts. Can you see why? You may wish to try implementing a nonblocking version like was done for fork.

```
def join[A](a: Par[Par[A]]): Par[A] =
  es => a(es).get.apply(es)

def joinViaFlatMap[A](a: Par[Par[A]]): Par[A] =
  flatMap(a)(a => a)

def flatMapViaJoin[A,B](p: Par[A])(f: A => Par[B]): Par[B] =
  join(map(p)(f))
```

Answers to exercises for chapter 8

Exercise 8.01

Here are a few properties:

- The sum of the empty list is 0.
- The sum of a list whose elements are all equal to x is just the list's length multiplied by x. We might express this as sum(List.fill(n)(x)) == n*x
- For any list, l, sum(l) == sum(l.reverse), since addition is commutative.
- Given a list, List(x,y,z,p,q), sum(List(x,y,z,p,q)) == sum(List(x,y)) + sum(List(z,p,q)), since addition is associative. More generally, we can partition a list into two subsequences whose sum is equal to the sum of the overall list.
- The sum of 1,2,3...n is n*(n+1)/2.

Exercise 8.02

- The max of a single element list is equal to that element.
- The max of a list is greater than or equal to all elements of the list.
- The max of a list is an element of that list.
- The max of the empty list is unspecified and should throw an error or return None.

Exercise 8.03

```
/* We can refer to the enclosing `Prop` instance with `Prop.this` */
def &&(p: Prop): Prop = new Prop {
  def check = Prop.this.check && p.check
}
```

Exercise 8.04

```
def choose(start: Int, stopExclusive: Int): Gen[Int] =
  Gen(State(RNG.nonNegativeInt).map(n => start + n % (stopExclusive-start)))

/* We could write this as an explicit state action, but this is far less
   convenient, since it requires us to manually thread the `RNG` through the
   computation. */
def choose2(start: Int, stopExclusive: Int): Gen[Int] =
  Gen(State(rng => RNG.nonNegativeInt(rng) match {
    case (n,rng2) => (start + n % (stopExclusive-start), rng2)
  }))
```

Exercise 8.05

```
def unit[A](a: => A): Gen[A] =
  Gen(State.unit(a))

def boolean: Gen[Boolean] =
  Gen(State(RNG.boolean))

def choose(start: Int, stopExclusive: Int): Gen[Int] =
  Gen(State(RNG.nonNegativeInt).map(n => start + n % (stopExclusive-start)))

def listOfN[A](n: Int, g: Gen[A]): Gen[List[A]] =
  Gen(State.sequence(List.fill(n)(g.sample)))
```

Exercise 8.06

These methods are defined in the Gen class:

```
def flatMap[B](f: A => Gen[B]): Gen[B] =
  Gen(sample.flatMap(a => f(a).sample))

/* A method alias for the function we wrote earlier. */
def listOfN(size: Int): Gen[List[A]] =
  Gen.listOfN(size, this)

/* A version of `listOfN` that generates the size to use dynamically. */
def listOfN(size: Gen[Int]): Gen[List[A]] =
  size flatMap (n => this.listOfN(n))
```

Exercise 8.07

```
def union[A](g1: Gen[A], g2: Gen[A]): Gen[A] =
  boolean.flatMap(b => if (b) g1 else g2)
```

Exercise 8.08

```
def weighted[A](g1: (Gen[A],Double), g2: (Gen[A],Double)): Gen[A] = {
  /* The probability we should pull from `g1`. */
  val g1Threshold = g1._2.abs / (g1._2.abs + g2._2.abs)

  Gen(State(RNG.double).flatMap(d =>
    if (d < g1Threshold) g1._1.sample else g2._1.sample))
}
```

Exercise 8.09

```
def &&(p: Prop) = Prop {
  (max,n,rng) => run(max,n,rng) match {
    case Passed => p.run(max, n, rng)
    case x => x
  }
}

def ||(p: Prop) = Prop {
  (max,n,rng) => run(max,n,rng) match {
    // In case of failure, run the other prop.
    case Falsified(msg, _) => p.tag(msg).run(max,n,rng)
    case x => x
  }
}
```

/* This is rather simplistic - in the event of failure, we simply prepend

```
 * the given message on a newline in front of the existing message.
 */
def tag(msg: String) = Prop {
  (max,n,rng) => run(max,n,rng) match {
    case Falsified(e, c) => Falsified(msg + "\n" + e, c)
    case x => x
  }
}
```

Exercise 8.10

```
def unsized: SGen[A] = SGen(_ => this)
```

Exercise 8.11

```
case class SGen[+A](g: Int => Gen[A]) {
  def apply(n: Int): Gen[A] = g(n)

  def map[B](f: A => B): SGen[B] =
    SGen(g andThen (_ map f))

  def flatMap[B](f: A => Gen[B]): SGen[B] =
    SGen(g andThen (_ flatMap f))

  def **[B](s2: SGen[B]): SGen[(A,B)] =
    SGen(n => apply(n) ** s2(n))
}
```

Exercise 8.12

```
def listOf[A](g: Gen[A]): SGen[List[A]] =
  SGen(n => g.listOfN(n))
```

Exercise 8.13

```
def listOf1[A](g: Gen[A]): SGen[List[A]] =
  SGen(n => g.listOfN(n max 1))

val maxProp1 = forAll(listOf1(smallInt)) { l =>
  val max = l.max
  !l.exists(_ > max) // No value greater than `max` should exist in `l`
}
```

Exercise 8.14

```
val sortedProp = forAll(listOf(smallInt)) { ns =>
  val nss = ns.sorted
  // We specify that every sorted list is either empty, has one element,
  // or has no two consecutive elements `(a,b)` such that `a` is greater than `b`.
  (ns.isEmpty || nss.tail.isEmpty || !ns.zip(ns.tail).exists {
    case (a,b) => a > b
  })
    // Also, the sorted list should have all the elements of the input list,
    && !ns.exists(!nss.contains(_))
    // and it should have no elements not in the input list.
    && !nss.exists(!ns.contains(_))
}
```

Exercise 8.15

A detailed answer is to be found in the file Exhaustive.scala in the code accompanying this chapter.

Exercise 8.16

```
/* A `Gen[Par[Int]]` generated from a list summation that spawns a new parallel
 * computation for each element of the input list summed to produce the final
 * result. This is not the most compelling example, but it provides at least some
 * variation in structure to use for testing.
 */
val pint2: Gen[Par[Int]] = choose(-100,100).listOfN(choose(0,20)).map(l =>
  l.foldLeft(Par.unit(0))((p,i) =>
    Par.fork { Par.map2(p, Par.unit(i))(_ + _) }))
```

Exercise 8.17

```
val forkProp = Prop.forAllPar(pint2)(i => equal(Par.fork(i), i)) tag "fork"
```

Exercise 8.18

- l.takeWhile(f) ++ l.dropWhile(f) == l
- We want to enforce that takeWhile returns the *longest* prefix whose elements satisfy the predicate. There are various ways to state this, but the general idea is that the remaining list, if non-empty, should start with an element that does *not* satisfy the predicate.

Answers to exercises for chapter 9

Exercise 9.01

```
def map2[A,B,C](p: Parser[A], p2: Parser[B])(
                f: (A,B) => C): Parser[C] =
  map(product(p, p2))(f.tupled)
def many1[A](p: Parser[A]): Parser[List[A]] =
  map2(p, many(p))(_ :: _)
```

Exercise 9.02

product is associative. These two expressions are "roughly" equal:

```
(a ** b) ** c
a ** (b ** c)
```

The only difference is how the pairs are nested. The (a ** b) ** c parser returns an ((A,B), C), whereas the a ** (b ** c) returns an (A, (B,C)). We can define functions unbiasL and unbiasR to convert these nested tuples to flat 3-tuples:

```
def unbiasL[A,B,C](p: ((A,B), C)): (A,B,C) = (p._1._1, p._1._2, p._2)
def unbiasR[A,B,C](p: (A, (B,C))): (A,B,C) = (p._1, p._2._1, p._2._2)
```

With these, we can now state the associativity property:

```
(a ** b) ** c map (unbiasL) == a ** (b ** c) map (unbiasR)
```

We'll sometimes just use ~= when there is an obvious bijection between the two sides:

```
(a ** b) ** c ~= a ** (b ** c)
```

`map` and `product` also have an interesting relationship–we can `map` either before or after taking the product of two parsers, without affecting the behavior:

```
a.map(f) ** b.map(g) == (a ** b) map { case (a,b) => (f(a), g(b)) }
```

For instance, if a and b were both `Parser[String]`, and f and g both computed the length of a string, it doesn't matter if we map over the result of a to compute its length, or whether we do that *after* the product.

See chapter 12 for more discussion of these laws.

Exercise 9.03

```
def many[A](p: Parser[A]): Parser[List[A]] =
  map2(p, many(p))(_ :: _) or succeed(List())
```

Exercise 9.04

```
def listOfN[A](n: Int, p: Parser[A]): Parser[List[A]] =
  if (n <= 0) succeed(List())
  else map2(p, listOfN(n-1, p))(_ :: _)
```

Exercise 9.05

We could introduce a combinator, `wrap`:

```
def wrap[A](p: => Parser[A]): Parser[A]
```

Then define `many` as:

```
def many[A](p: Parser[A]): Parser[List[A]] =
  map2(p, wrap(many(p)))(_ :: _) or succeed(List())
```

In the parallelism chapter, we were particularly interested in avoiding having `Par` objects that took as much time and space to build as the corresponding serial computation, and the `delay` combinator let us control this more carefully. Here, this isn't as much of a concern, and having to think carefully each time we `map2` to decide whether we need to call `wrap` seems like unnecessary friction for users of the API.

Exercise 9.06

We'll just have this parser return the number of `'a'` characters read. Note that we can declare a normal value inside a for-comprehension.

```
for {
  digit <- "[0-9]+".r
  val n = digit.toInt
  // we really should catch exceptions thrown by toInt
  // and convert to parse failure
  _ <- listOfN(n, char('a'))
} yield n
```

Exercise 9.07

These can be implemented using a for-comprehension, which delegates to the `flatMap` and `map` implementations we've provided on `ParserOps`, or they can be implemented in terms of these functions directly.

```
def product[A,B](p: Parser[A], p2: => Parser[B]): Parser[(A,B)] =
  flatMap(p)(a => map(p2)(b => (a,b)))

def map2[A,B,C](p: Parser[A], p2: => Parser[B])(f: (A,B) => C): Parser[C] =
  for { a <- p; b <- p2 } yield f(a,b)
```

Exercise 9.08

```
def map[A,B](p: Parser[A])(f: A => B): Parser[B] = p.flatMap(a => succeed(f(a)))
```

Exercise 9.09

See full implementation in JSON.scala[213].

Exercise 9.10

The next section works through a possible design in detail.

Exercise 9.11

---

[213]https://github.com/fpinscala/fpinscala/blob/master/answers/src/main/scala/fpinscala/parsing/JSON.scala

```
/**
 * In the event of an error, returns the error that occurred after consuming
 * the most number of characters.
 */
def furthest[A](p: Parser[A]): Parser[A]

/** In the event of an error, returns the error that occurred most recently. */
def latest[A](p: Parser[A]): Parser[A]
```

Exercise 9.12

Keep reading for a discussion

Exercise 9.13

There is a completed reference implementation of `Parsers` in parsing/instances/Reference.scala[214], though we recommend you continue reading before looking at that, since we're still refining the representation.

Exercise 9.14

Again, see `Reference.scala` for a fully worked implementation.

Exercise 9.15

Again see the reference implementation.

Exercise 9.16

```
case class ParseError(stack: List[(Location,String)] = List()) {
  def push(loc: Location, msg: String): ParseError =
    copy(stack = (loc,msg) :: stack)

  def label[A](s: String): ParseError =
    ParseError(latestLoc.map((_,s)).toList)

  def latest: Option[(Location,String)] =
    stack.lastOption

  def latestLoc: Option[Location] =
    latest map (_._1)
```

```scala
/**
Display collapsed error stack - any adjacent stack elements with the
same location are combined on one line. For the bottommost error, we
display the full line, with a caret pointing to the column of the error.
Example:

1.1 file 'companies.json'; array
5.1 object
5.2 key-value
5.10 ':'

{ "MSFT" ; 24,
         ^
*/
override def toString =
  if (stack.isEmpty) "no error message"
  else {
    val collapsed = collapseStack(stack)
    val context =
      collapsed.lastOption.map("\n\n" + _._1.currentLine).getOrElse("") +
      collapsed.lastOption.map("\n" + _._1.columnCaret).getOrElse("")
    collapsed.map {
      case (loc,msg) => loc.line.toString + "." + loc.col + " " + msg
    }.mkString("\n") + context
  }

/* Builds a collapsed version of the given error stack -
 * messages at the same location have their messages merged,
 * separated by semicolons */
def collapseStack(s: List[(Location,String)]): List[(Location,String)] =
  s.groupBy(_._1).
    mapValues(_.map(_._2).mkString("; ")).
    toList.sortBy(_._1.offset)

  def formatLoc(l: Location): String = l.line + "." + l.col
}
```

Exercise 9.17

See a fully worked implementation in instances/Sliceable.scala in the answers.

Exercise 9.18

We'll just give a sketch here. The basic idea is to add an additional field to ParseError:

```
case class ParseError(stack: List[(Location,String)] = List(),
                      otherFailures: List[ParseError] = List()) {

  def addFailure(e: ParseError): ParseError =
    this.copy(otherFailures = e :: this.otherFailures)
  ...
}
```

We then need to make sure we populate this in the implementation of or

```
def or[A](p: Parser[A], p2: => Parser[A]): Parser[A] =
  s => p(s) match {
    case Failure(e,false) => p2(s).mapError(_.addFailure(e))
    case r => r // committed failure or success skips running `p2`
  }
```

Of course, we have to decide how to print a ParseError for human consumption We also can expose combinators for selecting which error(s) get reported in the event that a chain of a | b | c fails—we might choose to collect up all the errors for each of the three parsers, or perhaps only show the parser that got the furthest in the input before failing, etc

Answers to exercises for chapter 10

Exercise 10.01

```
val intAddition: Monoid[Int] = new Monoid[Int] {
  def op(x: Int, y: Int) = x + y
  val zero = 0
}

val intMultiplication: Monoid[Int] = new Monoid[Int] {
  def op(x: Int, y: Int) = x * y
  val zero = 1
}

val booleanOr: Monoid[Boolean] = new Monoid[Boolean] {
  def op(x: Boolean, y: Boolean) = x || y
  val zero = false
}

val booleanAnd: Monoid[Boolean] = new Monoid[Boolean] {
  def op(x: Boolean, y: Boolean) = x && y
  val zero = true
}
```

Exercise 10.02

Notice that we have a choice in how we implement op. We can compose the options in either order. Both of those implementations satisfy the monoid laws, but they are not equivalent. This is true in general–that is, every monoid has a *dual* where the op combines things in the opposite order. Monoids like booleanOr and intAddition are equivalent to their duals because their op is commutative as well as associative.

```scala
def optionMonoid[A]: Monoid[Option[A]] = new Monoid[Option[A]] {
  def op(x: Option[A], y: Option[A]) = x orElse y
  val zero = None
}

// We can get the dual of any monoid just by flipping the `op`.
def dual[A](m: Monoid[A]): Monoid[A] = new Monoid[A] {
  def op(x: A, y: A): A = m.op(y, x)
  val zero = m.zero
}

// Now we can have both monoids on hand:
def firstOptionMonoid[A]: Monoid[Option[A]] = optionMonoid[A]
def lastOptionMonoid[A]: Monoid[Option[A]] = dual(firstOptionMonoid)
```

Exercise 10.03

There is a choice of implementation here as well. Do we implement it as f compose g or f andThen g? We have to pick one. We can then get the other one using the dual construct (see previous answer).

```scala
def endoMonoid[A]: Monoid[A => A] = new Monoid[A => A] {
  def op(f: A => A, g: A => A) = f compose g
  val zero = (a: A) => a
}
```

Exercise 10.04

```
import fpinscala.testing._
import Prop._

def monoidLaws[A](m: Monoid[A], gen: Gen[A]): Prop =
  // Associativity
  forAll(for {
    x <- gen
    y <- gen
    z <- gen
  } yield (x, y, z))(p =>
    m.op(p._1, m.op(p._2, p._3)) == m.op(m.op(p._1, p._2), p._3)) &&
  // Identity
  forAll(gen)((a: A) =>
    m.op(a, m.zero) == a && m.op(m.zero, a) == a)
```

Exercise 10.05

Notice that this function does not require the use of map at all.

```
def foldMap[A, B](as: List[A], m: Monoid[B])(f: A => B): B =
  as.foldLeft(m.zero)((b, a) => m.op(b, f(a)))
```

Exercise 10.06

The function type (A, B) => B, when curried, is A => (B => B). And of course, B => B is a monoid for any B (via function composition).

```
def foldRight[A, B](as: List[A])(z: B)(f: (A, B) => B): B =
  foldMap(as, endoMonoid[B])(f.curried)(z)
```

Folding to the left is the same except we flip the arguments to the function f to put the B on the correct side. Then we have to also "flip" the monoid so that it operates from left to right.

```
def foldLeft[A, B](as: List[A])(z: B)(f: (B, A) => B): B =
  foldMap(as, dual(endoMonoid[B]))(a => b => f(b, a))(z)
```

Exercise 10.07

```scala
def foldMapV[A, B](as: IndexedSeq[A], m: Monoid[B])(f: A => B): B =
  if (as.length == 0)
    m.zero
  else if (as.length == 1)
    f(as(0))
  else {
    val (l, r) = as.splitAt(as.length / 2)
    m.op(foldMapV(l, m)(f), foldMapV(r, m)(f))
  }
```

Exercise 10.08

```scala
// This ability to 'lift' a monoid any monoid to operate within
// some context (here `Par`) is something we'll discuss more in
// chapters 11 & 12
def par[A](m: Monoid[A]): Monoid[Par[A]] = new Monoid[Par[A]] {
  def zero = Par.unit(m.zero)
  def op(a: Par[A], b: Par[A]) = a.map2(b)(m.op)
}


// we perform the mapping and the reducing both in parallel
def parFoldMap[A,B](v: IndexedSeq[A], m: Monoid[B])(f: A => B): Par[B] =
  Par.parMap(v)(f).flatMap { bs =>
    foldMapV(bs, par(m))(b => Par.async(b))
  }
```

Exercise 10.09

```scala
// This implementation detects only ascending order,
// but you can write a monoid that detects both ascending and descending
// order if you like.
def ordered(ints: IndexedSeq[Int]): Boolean = {
  // Our monoid tracks the minimum and maximum element seen so far
  // as well as whether the elements are so far ordered.
  val mon = new Monoid[Option[(Int, Int, Boolean)]] {
    def op(o1: Option[(Int, Int, Boolean)], o2: Option[(Int, Int, Boolean)]) =
      (o1, o2) match {
        // The ranges should not overlap if the sequence is ordered.
        case (Some((x1, y1, p)), Some((x2, y2, q))) =>
          Some((x1 min x2, y1 max y2, p && q && y1 <= x2))
        case (x, None) => x
        case (None, x) => x
      }
    val zero = None
```

```
  }
  // The empty sequence is ordered, and each element by itself is ordered.
  foldMapV(ints, mon)(i => Some((i, i, true))).map(_._3).getOrElse(true)
}
```

Exercise 10.10

```
sealed trait WC
case class Stub(chars: String) extends WC
case class Part(lStub: String, words: Int, rStub: String) extends WC

val wcMonoid: Monoid[WC] = new Monoid[WC] {
  // The empty result, where we haven't seen any characters yet.
  val zero = Stub("")

  def op(a: WC, b: WC) = (a, b) match {
    case (Stub(c), Stub(d)) => Stub(c + d)
    case (Stub(c), Part(l, w, r)) => Part(c + l, w, r)
    case (Part(l, w, r), Stub(c)) => Part(l, w, r + c)
    case (Part(l1, w1, r1), Part(l2, w2, r2)) =>
      Part(l1, w1 + (if ((r1 + l2).isEmpty) 0 else 1) + w2, r2)
  }
}
```

Exercise 10.11

```
def count(s: String): Int = {
  def wc(c: Char): WC =
    if (c.isWhitespace)
      Part("", 0, "")
    else
      Stub(c.toString)
  def unstub(s: String) = s.length min 1
  foldMapV(s.toIndexedSeq, wcMonoid)(wc) match {
    case Stub(s) => unstub(s)
    case Part(l, w, r) => unstub(l) + w + unstub(r)
  }
}
```

Exercise 10.12

```scala
trait Foldable[F[_]] {
  def foldRight[A, B](as: F[A])(z: B)(f: (A, B) => B): B =
    foldMap(as)(f.curried)(endoMonoid[B])(z)

  def foldLeft[A, B](as: F[A])(z: B)(f: (B, A) => B): B =
    foldMap(as)(a => (b: B) => f(b, a))(dual(endoMonoid[B]))(z)

  def foldMap[A, B](as: F[A])(f: A => B)(mb: Monoid[B]): B =
    foldRight(as)(mb.zero)((a, b) => mb.op(f(a), b))

  def concatenate[A](as: F[A])(m: Monoid[A]): A =
    foldLeft(as)(m.zero)(m.op)
}

object ListFoldable extends Foldable[List] {
  override def foldRight[A, B](as: List[A])(z: B)(f: (A, B) => B) =
    as.foldRight(z)(f)
  override def foldLeft[A, B](as: List[A])(z: B)(f: (B, A) => B) =
    as.foldLeft(z)(f)
  override def foldMap[A, B](as: List[A])(f: A => B)(mb: Monoid[B]): B =
    foldLeft(as)(mb.zero)((b, a) => mb.op(b, f(a)))
}

object IndexedSeqFoldable extends Foldable[IndexedSeq] {
  import Monoid._
  override def foldRight[A, B](as: IndexedSeq[A])(z: B)(f: (A, B) => B) =
    as.foldRight(z)(f)
  override def foldLeft[A, B](as: IndexedSeq[A])(z: B)(f: (B, A) => B) =
    as.foldLeft(z)(f)
  override def foldMap[A, B](as: IndexedSeq[A])(f: A => B)(mb: Monoid[B]): B =
    foldMapV(as, mb)(f)
}

object StreamFoldable extends Foldable[Stream] {
  override def foldRight[A, B](as: Stream[A])(z: B)(f: (A, B) => B) =
    as.foldRight(z)(f)
  override def foldLeft[A, B](as: Stream[A])(z: B)(f: (B, A) => B) =
    as.foldLeft(z)(f)
}
```

Exercise 10.13

```
sealed trait Tree[+A]
case class Leaf[A](value: A) extends Tree[A]
case class Branch[A](left: Tree[A], right: Tree[A]) extends Tree[A]

object TreeFoldable extends Foldable[Tree] {
  override def foldMap[A, B](as: Tree[A])(f: A => B)(mb: Monoid[B]): B =
    as match {
      case Leaf(a) => f(a)
      case Branch(l, r) => mb.op(foldMap(l)(f)(mb), foldMap(r)(f)(mb))
    }
  override def foldLeft[A, B](as: Tree[A])(z: B)(f: (B, A) => B) = as match {
    case Leaf(a) => f(z, a)
    case Branch(l, r) => foldLeft(r)(foldLeft(l)(z)(f))(f)
  }
  override def foldRight[A, B](as: Tree[A])(z: B)(f: (A, B) => B) = as match {
    case Leaf(a) => f(a, z)
    case Branch(l, r) => foldRight(l)(foldRight(r)(z)(f))(f)
  }
}
```

Notice that in `TreeFoldable.foldMap`, we don't actually use the `zero` from the `Monoid`. This is because there is no empty tree. This suggests that there might be a class of types that are foldable with something "smaller" than a monoid, consisting only of an associative `op`. That kind of object (a monoid without a zero) is called a *semigroup*.

Exercise 10.14

```
object OptionFoldable extends Foldable[Option] {
  override def foldMap[A, B](as: Option[A])(f: A => B)(mb: Monoid[B]): B =
    as match {
      case None => mb.zero
      case Some(a) => f(a)
    }
  override def foldLeft[A, B](as: Option[A])(z: B)(f: (B, A) => B) = as match {
    case None => z
    case Some(a) => f(z, a)
  }
  override def foldRight[A, B](as: Option[A])(z: B)(f: (A, B) => B) = as match {
    case None => z
    case Some(a) => f(a, z)
  }
}
```

Exercise 10.15

```
def toList[A](as: F[A]): List[A] =
  foldRight(as)(List[A]())(_ :: _)
```

Exercise 10.16

```
def productMonoid[A,B](A: Monoid[A], B: Monoid[B]): Monoid[(A, B)] =
  new Monoid[(A, B)] {
    def op(x: (A, B), y: (A, B)) =
      (A.op(x._1, y._1), B.op(x._2, y._2))
    val zero = (A.zero, B.zero)
  }
```

Exercise 10.17

```
def functionMonoid[A,B](B: Monoid[B]): Monoid[A => B] =
  new Monoid[A => B] {
    def op(f: A => B, g: A => B) = a => B.op(f(a), g(a))
    val zero: A => B = a => B.zero
  }
```

Exercise 10.18

```
def mapMergeMonoid[K,V](V: Monoid[V]): Monoid[Map[K, V]] =
  new Monoid[Map[K, V]] {
    def zero = Map[K,V]()
    def op(a: Map[K, V], b: Map[K, V]) =
      (a.keySet ++ b.keySet).foldLeft(zero) { (acc,k) =>
        acc.updated(k, V.op(a.getOrElse(k, V.zero),
                            b.getOrElse(k, V.zero)))
      }
  }

def bag[A](as: IndexedSeq[A]): Map[A, Int] =
  foldMapV(as, mapMergeMonoid[A, Int](intAddition))((a: A) => Map(a -> 1))
```

Answers to exercises for chapter 11

Exercise 11.01

```
val parMonad = new Monad[Par] {
  def unit[A](a: => A) = Par.unit(a)
  def flatMap[A,B](ma: Par[A])(f: A => Par[B]) = Par.flatMap(ma)(f)
}

def parserMonad[P[+_]](p: Parsers[P]) = new Monad[P] {
  def unit[A](a: => A) = p.succeed(a)
  def flatMap[A,B](ma: P[A])(f: A => P[B]) = p.flatMap(ma)(f)
}

val optionMonad = new Monad[Option] {
  def unit[A](a: => A) = Some(a)
  def flatMap[A,B](ma: Option[A])(f: A => Option[B]) = ma flatMap f
}

val streamMonad = new Monad[Stream] {
  def unit[A](a: => A) = Stream(a)
  def flatMap[A,B](ma: Stream[A])(f: A => Stream[B]) = ma flatMap f
}

val listMonad = new Monad[List] {
  def unit[A](a: => A) = List(a)
  def flatMap[A,B](ma: List[A])(f: A => List[B]) = ma flatMap f
}
```

Exercise 11.02

Since State is a binary type constructor, we need to partially apply it with the S type argument. Thus, it is not just one monad, but an entire family of monads, one for each type S. One solution is to create a class StateMonads that accepts the S type argument and then has a *type member* for the fully applied State[S, A] type inside:

```
class StateMonads[S] {
  type StateS[A] = State[S, A]

  // We can then declare the monad for the `StateS` type constructor:
  val monad = new Monad[StateS] {
    def unit[A](a: => A): State[S, A] = State(s => (a, s))
    override def flatMap[A,B](st: State[S, A])(f: A => State[S, B]): State[S, B] =
      st flatMap f
  }
}
```

But we don't have to create a full class like StateMonads. We can create an anonymous class inline, inside parentheses, and project out its type member f. This is sometimes called a "type lambda", since it's very similar to a type-level anonymous function.

```scala
def stateMonad[S] = new Monad[({type f[x] = State[S, x]})#f] {
  def unit[A](a: => A): State[S, A] = State(s => (a, s))
  override def flatMap[A,B](st: State[S, A])(f: A => State[S, B]): State[S, B] =
    st flatMap f
}
```

Exercise 11.03

```scala
def sequence[A](lma: List[F[A]]): F[List[A]] =
  lma.foldRight(unit(List[A]()))((ma, mla) => map2(ma, mla)(_ :: _))


def traverse[A,B](la: List[A])(f: A => F[B]): F[List[B]] =
  la.foldRight(unit(List[B]()))((a, mlb) => map2(f(a), mlb)(_ :: _))


/**
 * 'Balanced' sequencing, which should behave like `sequence`,
 * but it can use less stack for some data types. We'll see later
 * in this chapter how the monad _laws_ let us conclude both
 * definitions 'mean' the same thing.
 */
def bsequence[A](ms: Seq[F[A]]): F[IndexedSeq[A]] = {
  if (ms.isEmpty) point(Vector())
  else if (ms.size == 1) ms.head.map(Vector(_))
  else {
    val (l,r) = ms.toIndexedSeq.splitAt(ms.length / 2)
    map2(bsequence(l), bsequence(r))(_ ++ _)
  }
}
```

Exercise 11.04

```scala
// Recursive version:
def _replicateM[A](n: Int, ma: F[A]): F[List[A]] =
  if (n <= 0) unit(List[A]()) else map2(ma, replicateM(n - 1, ma))(_ :: _)

// Using `sequence` and the `List.fill` function of the standard library:
def replicateM[A](n: Int, ma: F[A]): F[List[A]] =
  sequence(List.fill(n)(ma))
```

Exercise 11.05

For List, the replicateM function will generate a list of lists. It will contain all the lists of length n with elements selected from the input list.

For Option, it will generate either Some or None based on whether the input is Some or None. The Some case will contain a list of length n that repeats the element in the input Option.

The general meaning of replicateM is described well by the implementation sequence(List.fill(n)(ma)). It repeats the ma monadic value n times and gathers the results in a single value, where the monad F determines how values are actually combined.

Exercise 11.06

For Par, filterM filters a list, applying the functions in parallel; for Option, it filters a list, but allows the filtering function to fail and abort the filter computation; for Gen, it produces a generator for subsets of the input list, where the function f picks a 'weight' for each element (in the form of a Gen[Boolean])

```
def filterM[A](ms: List[A])(f: A => F[Boolean]): F[List[A]] =
  ms match {
    case Nil => unit(Nil)
    case h :: t => flatMap(f(h))(b =>
      if (!b) filterM(t)(f)
      else map(filterM(t)(f))(h :: _))
  }
```

Exercise 11.07

```
def compose[A,B,C](f: A => F[B], g: B => F[C]): A => F[C] =
  a => flatMap(f(a))(g)
```

Exercise 11.08

```
def flatMap[A,B](ma: F[A])(f: A => F[B]): F[B] =
  compose((_:Unit) => ma, f)(())
```

Exercise 11.09

Let's rewrite the following in terms of flatMap:

```
compose(compose(f, g), h) == compose(f, compose(g, h))

a => flatMap(compose(f, g)(a))(h) == a => flatMap(f(a))(compose(g, h))

a => flatMap((b => flatMap(f(b))(g))(a))(h) ==
  a => flatMap(f(a))(b => flatMap(g(b))(h))
```

So far we have just expanded the definition of compose. Equals substituted for equals. Let's simplify the left side a little:

```
a => flatMap(flatMap(f(a))(g))(h) == a => flatMap(f(a))(b => flatMap(g(b))(h))
```

Let's simplify again by eliminating the a argument and substituting a hypothetical value x for f(a):

```
flatMap(flatMap(x)(g))(h) == flatMap(x)(b => flatMap(g(b))(h))
```

This now looks exactly like the monad law stated in terms of flatMap, just with different names:

```
flatMap(flatMap(x)(f))(g) == flatMap(x)(a => flatMap(f(a))(g))
```

Q.E.D.

Exercise 11.10

We simply substitute the definition of compose in terms of flatMap.

```
compose(f, unit)(v) == f(v)              // for all functions f and values v
(a => flatMap(f(a))(unit))(v) == f(v)    // Expand `compose`
flatMap(f(v))(unit) == f(v)              // Simplify function application
flatMap(x)(unit) == x                    // Abstract out `f(v)`

compose(unit, f)(x) == f(x)
flatMap(unit(x))(f) == f(x)  // Expand `compose`
```

Q.E.D.

Exercise 11.11

For Option, we again consider both cases None and Some and expand the equation. The monadic unit is the Some(_) constructor.

```
// Left identity is trivially true for None:
flatMap(None)(Some(_)) == None

// And here it is for Some:
flatMap(Some(v))(Some(_)) == Some(v)
// Substitute the definition of `flatMap`:
Some(v) == Some(v)

// Right identity is just as easy for None:
flatMap(Some(None))(f) == f(None)
// Substitute definition of flatMap:
f(None) == f(None)

// And for Some:
flatMap(Some(Some(v)))(f) == f(Some(v))
// Substitute definition of flatMap:
f(Some(v)) == f(Some(v))
```

Exercise 11.12

```
def join[A](mma: F[F[A]]): F[A] = flatMap(mma)(ma => ma)
```

Exercise 11.13

```
def flatMap[A,B](ma: F[A])(f: A => F[B]) =
  join(map(ma)(f))

def compose[A,B,C](f: A => F[B], g: B => F[C]): A => F[C] =
  a => join(map(f(a))(g))
```

Exercise 11.14

We can look at the associative law in terms of `flatMap` from another perspective. It says that `x.flatMap(f).flatMap(g)` is equal to `x.flatMap(a => f(a).flatMap(g))` *for all* choices of `f` and `g`. So let's pick a particular `f` and `g` that's easy to think about. We can just pick the identity function:

```
x.flatMap(z => z).flatMap(z => z) == x.flatMap(a => a.flatMap(z => z))
```

And of course, flatMapping with the identify function is `join`! The associative law can now be stated as:

```
join(join(x)) == x.flatMap(join)
```

And we know that `flatMap` is "map, then join," so let's eliminate this last call to `flatMap`:

```
join(join(x)) == join(map(x)(join))
```

The identity laws in terms of `join` are:

```
join(map(x)(unit)) == x
join(unit(x)) == x
```

This follows from the definition of `join` and the identity laws in terms of `flatMap`:

```
flatMap(x)(unit) == x
flatMap(unit(x))(f) == f(x)
```

For the second law, we simply substitute the identity function for `f`, which gives us `join`.

Let's make a fast-and-loose proof for this version of the associative law using the `List` monad as an example. Of course, `join` in the `List` monad is just *list concatenation*:

```
scala> listMonad.join(List(List(1, 2), List(3, 4)))
res0: List[Int] = List(1, 2, 3, 4)
```

Now let's say we have some lists, nested to a depth of three:

```
val ns: List[List[List[Int]]] =
  List(List(List(1,2), List(3,4)),
       List(List(), List(5)))
```

If we `join` this list, the outer lists get concatenated and we have a list of lists two levels deep:

```
scala> ns.flatten
res1: List[List[Int]] = List(List(1, 2), List(3, 4), List(), List(5))
```

If we instead *map* join over it, we get a different nesting but again two levels deep. This flattens the *inner* lists.

```
scala> ns.map(listMonad.join)
res2: List[List[Int]] = List(List(1, 2, 3, 4), List(5))
```

And then joining res1 should be the same as joining res2:

```
scala> listMonad.join(res1) == listMonad.join(res2)
res3: Boolean = true
```

So all that the associative law is saying for the List monad is that concatenating the outer lists and then the inner ones (join(join(ns))) is the same as first concatenating the inner lists and then the outer ones (join(ns.map(join))).

Exercise 11.15

We can state the associative law in terms of join:

```
join(join(x)) == join(map(x)(join))
```

For Par, the join combinator means something like "make the outer thread wait for the inner one to finish." What this law is saying is that if you have threads starting threads three levels deep, then joining the inner threads and then the outer ones is the same as joining the outer threads and then the inner ones.

For Parser, the join combinator is running the outer parser to produce a Parser, then running the inner Parser *on the remaining input*. The associative law is saying, roughly, that only the *order* of nesting matters, since that's what affects the order in which the parsers are run.

Exercise 11.16

Recall the identity laws:

- left identity: flatMap(unit(x))(f) == f(x)
- right identity: flatMap(x)(unit) == x

The left identity law for Gen: The law states that if you take the values generated by unit(x) (which are always x) and apply f to those values, that's exactly the same as the generator returned by f(x).

The right identity law for Gen: The law states that if you apply unit to the values inside the generator x, that does not in any way differ from x itself.

The left identity law for List: The law says that wrapping a list in a singleton List and then flattening the result is the same as doing nothing.

The right identity law for List: The law says that if you take every value in a list, wrap each one in a singleton List, and then flatten the result, you get the list you started with.

Exercise 11.17

```
case class Id[A](value: A) {
  def map[B](f: A => B): Id[B] = Id(f(value))
  def flatMap[B](f: A => Id[B]): Id[B] = f(value)
}

object Id {
  val idMonad = new Monad[Id] {
    def unit[A](a: => A) = Id(a)
    def flatMap[A,B](ida: Id[A])(f: A => Id[B]): Id[B] = ida flatMap f
  }
}
```

Exercise 11.18

replicateM for State repeats the same state transition a number of times and returns a list of the results. It's not passing the same starting state many times, but chaining the calls together so that the output state of one is the input state of the next.

map2 works similarly in that it takes two state transitions and feeds the output state of one to the input of the other. The outputs are not put in a list, but combined with a function f.

sequence takes an entire list of state transitions and does the same kind of thing as replicateM: it feeds the output state of the first state transition to the input state of the next, and so on. The results are accumulated in a list.

Exercise 11.19

```
// Getting and setting the same state does nothing:
getState.flatMap(setState) == unit(())

// written as for-comprehension:
for {
  x <- getState
  _ <- setState(x)
} yield ()

// Setting the state to `s` and getting it back out yields `s`.
setState(s).flatMap(_ => getState) == unit(s)

// alternatively:
for {
  _ <- setState(s)
  x <- getState
} yield x
```

Exercise 11.20

```
object Reader {
  def readerMonad[R] = new Monad[({type f[x] = Reader[R,x]})#f] {
    def unit[A](a: => A): Reader[R,A] = Reader(_ => a)
    def flatMap[A,B](st: Reader[R,A])(f: A => Reader[R,B]): Reader[R,B] =
      Reader(r => f(st.run(r)).run(r))
  }

  // A primitive operation for it would be simply to ask for the `R` argument:
  def ask[R]: Reader[R, R] = Reader(r => r)
}
```

The action of Reader's `flatMap` is to pass the `r` argument along to both the outer Reader and also to the result of `f`, the inner Reader. Similar to how `State` passes along a state, except that in `Reader` the "state" is read-only.

The meaning of `sequence` here is that if you have a list of functions, you can turn it into a function that takes one argument and passes it to all the functions in the list, returning a list of the results.

The meaning of `join` is simply to pass the same value as both arguments to a binary function.

The meaning of `replicateM` is to apply the same function a number of times to the same argument, returning a list of the results. Note that if this function is *pure*, (which it should be), this can be exploited by only applying the function once and replicating the result instead of calling the function many times. This means the Reader monad can override replicateM to provide a very efficient implementation.

Answers to exercises for chapter 12

Exercise 12.01

```
def sequence[A](fas: List[F[A]]): F[List[A]] =
  traverse(fas)(fa => fa)

def replicateM[A](n: Int, fa: F[A]): F[List[A]] =
  sequence(List.fill(n)(fa))

def product[A,B](fa: F[A], fb: F[B]): F[(A,B)] =
  map2(fa, fb)((_,_))
```

Exercise 12.02

```
trait Applicative[F[_]] extends Functor[F] {
  // `map2` is implemented by first currying `f` so we get a function
  // of type `A => B => C`. This is a function that takes `A` and returns
  // another function of type `B => C`. So if we map `f.curried` over an
  // `F[A]`, we get `F[B => C]`. Passing that to `apply` along with the
  // `F[B]` will give us the desired `F[C]`.
  def map2[A,B,C](fa: F[A], fb: F[B])(f: (A, B) => C): F[C] =
    apply(map(fa)(f.curried), fb)


  // We simply use `map2` to lift a function into `F` so we can apply it
  // to both `fab` and `fa`. The function being lifted here is `_(_)`,
  // which is the same as the lambda notation `(f, x) => f(x)`. That is,
  // It's a function that takes two arguments:
  //   1. A function `f`
  //   2. An argument `x` to that function
  // and it simply applies `f` to `x`.
  def apply[A,B](fab: F[A => B])(fa: F[A]): F[B] =
    map2(fab, fa)(_(_))
  def unit[A](a: => A): F[A]


  def map[A,B](fa: F[A])(f: A => B): F[B] =
    apply(unit(f))(fa)
}
```

Exercise 12.03

```
/*
The pattern is simple. We just curry the function
we want to lift, pass the result to `unit`, and then `apply`
as many times as there are arguments.
Each call to `apply` is a partial application of the function
*/
def map3[A,B,C,D](fa: F[A],
                  fb: F[B],
                  fc: F[C])(f: (A, B, C) => D): F[D] =
  apply(apply(apply(unit(f.curried))(fa))(fb))(fc)

def map4[A,B,C,D,E](fa: F[A],
                    fb: F[B],
                    fc: F[C],
                    fd: F[D])(f: (A, B, C, D) => E): F[E]
  apply(apply(apply(apply(unit(f.curried))(fa))(fb))(fc))(fd)
```

Exercise 12.04

This transposes the list! That is, we start with a list of rows, each of which is possibly infinite in length. We get back a single row, where each element is the column of values at that position. Try it yourself in the REPL.

Exercise 12.05

```
def eitherMonad[E]: Monad[({type f[x] = Either[E, x]})#f] =
  new Monad[({type f[x] = Either[E, x]})#f] {
    def unit[A](a: => A): Either[E, A] = Right(a)
    def flatMap[A,B](eea: Either[E, A])(f: A => Either[E, B]) = eea match {
      case Right(a) => f(a)
      case Left(e) => Left(e)
    }
  }
```

Exercise 12.06

```
def validationApplicative[E]: Applicative[({type f[x] = Validation[E,x]})#f] =
  new Applicative[({type f[x] = Validation[E,x]})#f] {
    def unit[A](a: => A) = Success(a)
    override def map2[A,B,C](fa: Validation[E,A],
                            fb: Validation[E,B])(f: (A, B) => C) =
      (fa, fb) match {
        case (Success(a), Success(b)) => Success(f(a, b))
        case (Failure(h1, t1), Failure(h2, t2)) =>
          Failure(h1, t1 ++ Vector(h2) ++ t2)
        case (e@Failure(_, _), _) => e
        case (_, e@Failure(_, _)) => e
      }
  }
```

Exercise 12.07

We'll just work through left and right identity, but the basic idea for all these proofs is to substitute the definition of all functions, then use the monad laws to make simplifications to the applicative identities.

Let's start with left and right identity:

```
map2(unit(()), fa)((_,a) => a) == fa // Left identity
map2(fa, unit(()))((a,_) => a) == fa // Right identity
```

We'll do left identity first. We expand definition of map2:

```
def map2[A,B,C](fa: F[A], fb: F[B])(f: (A,B) => C): F[C]
  flatMap(fa)(a => map(fb)(b => f(a,b)))
```

```
flatMap(unit())(u => map(fa)(a => a)) == fa
```

We just substituted unit(()) and (_,a) => a in for f. map(fa)(a => a) is just fa by the functor laws, giving us:

```
flatMap(unit())(u => fa) == fa
```

Recall that flatMap can be rewritten using compose, by using Unit as the argument to the first function.

```
compose(unit, u => fa)(()) == fa
```

And by the monad laws:

```
compose(unit, f) == f
```

Therefore, compose(unit, u => fa) simplifies to u => fa. And u is just Unit here, and is ignored, so this is equivalent to fa:

```
(u => fa)(()) == fa
fa == fa
```

Right identity is symmetric; we just end up using the other identity for compose, that compose(f, unit) == f.

```
flatMap(fa)(a => map(unit(()))(u => a)) == fa
flatMap(fa)(a => unit(a)) == fa  // via functor laws
compose(u => fa, unit)(()) == fa
(u => fa)(()) == fa
fa == fa
```

Associativity and naturality are left as an exercise.

Exercise 12.08

```
def product[G[_]](G: Applicative[G]): Applicative[({type f[x] = (F[x], G[x])})#f] = {
  val self = this
  new Applicative[({type f[x] = (F[x], G[x])})#f] {
    def unit[A](a: => A) = (self.unit(a), G.unit(a))
    override def apply[A,B](fs: (F[A => B], G[A => B]))(p: (F[A], G[A])) =
      (self.apply(fs._1)(p._1), G.apply(fs._2)(p._2))
  }
}
```

Exercise 12.09

```
def compose[G[_]](G: Applicative[G]): Applicative[({type f[x] = F[G[x]]})#f] = {
  val self = this
  new Applicative[({type f[x] = F[G[x]]})#f] {
    def unit[A](a: => A) = self.unit(G.unit(a))
    override def map2[A,B,C](fga: F[G[A]], fgb: F[G[B]])(f: (A,B) => C) =
      self.map2(fga, fgb)(G.map2(_,_)(f))
  }
}
```

Exercise 12.10

If `self` and `G` both satisfy the laws, then so does the composite. The full proof of the laws can be found at: https://github.com/runarorama/sannanir/blob/master/Applicative.v

Exercise 12.11

You want to try writing `flatMap` in terms of `Monad[F]` and `Monad[G]`.

```
def flatMap[A,B](mna: F[G[A]])(f: A => F[G[B]]): F[G[B]] =
  self.flatMap(na => G.flatMap(na)(a => ???))
```

Here all you have is `f`, which returns an `F[G[B]]`. For it to have the appropriate type to return from the argument to `G.flatMap`, you'd need to be able to "swap" the `F` and `G` types. In other words, you'd need a *distributive law*. Such an operation is not part of the `Monad` interface.

Exercise 12.12

```
def sequenceMap[K,V](ofa: Map[K,F[V]]): F[Map[K,V]] =
  (ofa foldLeft unit(Map.empty[K,V])) {
    case (acc, (k, fv)) =>
      map2(acc, fv)((m, v) => m + (k -> v))
  }
```

Exercise 12.13

```
val listTraverse = new Traverse[List] {
  override def traverse[G[_],A,B](as: List[A])(
    f: A => G[B])(implicit G: Applicative[G]): G[List[B]] =
      as.foldRight(G.unit(List[B]()))((a, fbs) => G.map2(f(a), fbs)(_ :: _))
}

val optionTraverse = new Traverse[Option] {
  override def traverse[G[_],A,B](oa: Option[A])(
    f: A => G[B])(implicit G: Applicative[G]): G[Option[B]] =
      oa match {
        case Some(a) => G.map(f(a))(Some(_))
        case None    => G.unit(None)
      }
}

val treeTraverse = new Traverse[Tree] {
  override def traverse[G[_],A,B](ta: Tree[A])(
    f: A => G[B])(implicit G: Applicative[G]): G[Tree[B]] =
      G.map2(f(ta.head),
             listTraverse.traverse(ta.tail)(a => traverse(a)(f)))(Tree(_, _))
}
```

Exercise 12.14

The simplest possible `Applicative` we can use is `Id`:

```
type Id[A] = A
```

We already know this forms a `Monad`, so it's also an applicative functor:

```
val idMonad = new Monad[Id] {
  def unit[A](a: => A) = a
  override def flatMap[A,B](a: A)(f: A => B): B = f(a)
}
```

We can now implement `map` by calling `traverse`, picking `Id` as the `Applicative`:

```
def map[A,B](fa: F[A])(f: A => B): F[B] =
  traverse[Id, A, B](xs)(f)(idMonad)
```

This implementation is suggestive of laws for traverse, since we expect this implementation to obey the usual functor laws. See the chapter notes for discussion of the laws for Traverse.

Note that we can define traverse in terms of sequence and map, which means that a valid Traverse instance may define sequence and map, or just traverse:

```
trait Traverse[F[_]] extends Functor[F] {
  def traverse[G[_]:Applicative,A,B](fa: F[A])(f: A => G[B]): G[F[B]] =
    sequence(map(fa)(f))
  def sequence[G[_]:Applicative,A](fga: F[G[A]]): G[F[A]] =
    traverse(fga)(ga => ga)
  def map[A,B](fa: F[A])(f: A => B): F[B] =
    traverse[Id, A, B](fa)(f)(idMonad)
}
```

Exercise 12.15

It's because foldRight, foldLeft, and foldMap don't give us any way of constructing a value of the foldable type. In order to map over a structure, you need the ability to create a new structure (such as Nil and Cons in the case of a List). Traverse is able to extend Functor precisely because a traversal preserves the original structure. An example of a Foldable that is not a functor:

```
case class Iteration[A](a: A, f: A => A, n: Int) {
  def foldMap[B](g: A => B)(M: Monoid[B]): B = {
    def iterate(n: Int, b: B, c: A): B =
      if (n <= 0) b else iterate(n-1, g(c), f(a))
    iterate(n, M.zero, a)
  }
}
```

This class conceptually represents a sequence of A values, generated by repeated function application starting from some seed value. But can you see why it's not possible to define map for this type?

Exercise 12.16

```
def reverse[A](fa: F[A]): F[A] =
  mapAccum(fa, toList(fa).reverse)((_, as) => (as.head, as.tail))._1
```

Exercise 12.17

```
override def foldLeft[A,B](fa: F[A])(z: B)(f: (B, A) => B): B =
  mapAccum(fa, z)((a, b) => ((), f(b, a)))._2
```

Exercise 12.18

```
def fuse[G[_],H[_],A,B](fa: F[A])(f: A => G[B], g: A => H[B])
                       (implicit G: Applicative[G],
                                 H: Applicative[H]): (G[F[B]], H[F[B]]) =
  traverse[({type f[x] = (G[x], H[x])})#f, A, B](fa)(a => (f(a), g(a)))(G product H)
```

Exercise 12.19

```
def compose[G[_]](implicit G: Traverse[G]): Traverse[({type f[x] = F[G[x]]})#f] =
  new Traverse[({type f[x] = F[G[x]]})#f] {
    override def traverse[M[_]:Applicative,A,B](fa: F[G[A]])(f: A => M[B]) =
      self.traverse(fa)((ga: G[A]) => G.traverse(ga)(f))
  }
```

Exercise 12.20

```
def composeM[G[_],H[_]](implicit G: Monad[G], H: Monad[H], T: Traverse[H]):
  Monad[({type f[x] = G[H[x]]})#f] = new Monad[({type f[x] = G[H[x]]})#f] {
    def unit[A](a: => A): G[H[A]] = G.unit(H.unit(a))
    override def flatMap[A,B](mna: G[H[A]])(f: A => G[H[B]]): G[H[B]] =
      G.flatMap(mna)(na => G.map(T.traverse(na)(f))(H.join))
  }
```

Answers to exercises for chapter 13

Exercise 13.01

```
def freeMonad[F[_]]: Monad[({type f[a] = Free[F,a]})#f] =
  new Monad[({type f[a] = Free[F,a]})#f] {
    def unit[A](a: => A) = Return(a)
    def flatMap[A,B](fa: Free[F, A])(f: A => Free[F, B]) = fa flatMap f
  }
```

Exercise 13.02

```
@annotation.tailrec
def runTrampoline[A](a: Free[Function0,A]): A = (a) match {
  case Return(a) => a
  case Suspend(r) => r()
  case FlatMap(x,f) => x match {
    case Return(a) => runTrampoline { f(a) }
    case Suspend(r) => runTrampoline { f(r()) }
    case FlatMap(a0,g) => runTrampoline { a0 flatMap { a0 => g(a0) flatMap f } }
  }
}
```

Exercise 13.03

```
// Exercise 3: Implement a `Free` interpreter which works for any `Monad`
def run[F[_],A](a: Free[F,A])(implicit F: Monad[F]): F[A] = step(a) match {
  case Return(a) => F.unit(a)
  case Suspend(r) => r
  case FlatMap(Suspend(r), f) => F.flatMap(r)(a => run(f(a)))
  case _ => sys.error("Impossible, since `step` eliminates these cases")
}
```

Exercise 13.04

```
def translate[F[_],G[_],A](f: Free[F,A])(fg: F ~> G): Free[G,A] = {
  type FreeG[A] = Free[G,A]
  val t = new (F ~> FreeG) {
    def apply[A](a: F[A]): Free[G,A] = Suspend { fg(a) }
  }
  runFree(f)(t)(freeMonad[G])
}

def runConsole[A](a: Free[Console,A]): A =
  runTrampoline { translate(a)(new (Console ~> Function0) {
    def apply[A](c: Console[A]) = c.toThunk
  })}
```

Exercise 13.05

```
/*
 * Exercise 5: Implement a non-blocking read from an asynchronous file channel.
 * We'll just give the basic idea - here, we construct a `Future`
 * by reading from an `AsynchronousFileChannel`, a `java.nio` class
 * which supports asynchronous reads.
 */

import java.nio._
import java.nio.channels._

def read(file: AsynchronousFileChannel,
         fromPosition: Long,
         numBytes: Int): Par[Either[Throwable, Array[Byte]]] =
  Par.async { (cb: Either[Throwable, Array[Byte]] => Unit) =>
    val buf = ByteBuffer.allocate(numBytes)
    file.read(buf, fromPosition, (), new CompletionHandler[Integer, Unit] {
      def completed(bytesRead: Integer, ignore: Unit) = {
        val arr = new Array[Byte](bytesRead)
        buf.slice.get(arr, 0, bytesRead)
        cb(Right(arr))
      }
      def failed(err: Throwable, ignore: Unit) =
        cb(Left(err))
    })
  }

// note: We can wrap `read` in `Free[Par,A]` using the `Suspend` constructor
```

Answers to exercises for chapter 14

Exercise 14.01

```
def fill(xs: Map[Int,A]): ST[S,Unit] =
  xs.foldRight(ST[S,Unit](())) {
    case ((k, v), st) => st flatMap (_ => write(k, v))
  }
```

Exercise 14.02

```scala
// An action that does nothing
def noop[S] = ST[S,Unit](())

def partition[S](a: STArray[S,Int], l: Int, r: Int, pivot: Int): ST[S,Int] =
  for {
    vp <- a.read(pivot)
    _ <- a.swap(pivot, r)
    j <- STRef(l)
    _ <- (l until r).foldLeft(noop[S])((s, i) => for {
      _ <- s
      vi <- a.read(i)
      _ <- if (vi < vp) (for {
        vj <- j.read
        _ <- a.swap(i, vj)
        _ <- j.write(vj + 1)
      } yield ()) else noop[S]
    } yield ())
    x <- j.read
    _ <- a.swap(x, r)
  } yield x

def qs[S](a: STArray[S,Int], l: Int, r: Int): ST[S, Unit] = if (l < r) for {
  pi <- partition(a, l, r, l + (r - 1) / 2)
  _ <- qs(a, l, pi - 1)
  _ <- qs(a, pi + 1, r)
} yield () else noop[S]
```

Exercise 14.03

```scala
import scala.collection.mutable.HashMap

sealed trait STMap[S,K,V] {
  protected def table: HashMap[K,V]

  def size: ST[S,Int] = ST(table.size)

  // Get the value under a key
  def apply(k: K): ST[S,V] = ST(table(k))

  // Get the value under a key, or None if the key does not exist
  def get(k: K): ST[S, Option[V]] = ST(table.get(k))

  // Add a value under a key
  def +=(kv: (K, V)): ST[S,Unit] = ST(table += kv)
```

```
  // Remove a key
  def -=(k: K): ST[S,Unit] = ST(table -= k)
}

object STMap {
  def empty[S,K,V]: ST[S, STMap[S,K,V]] = ST(new STMap[S,K,V] {
    val table = HashMap.empty[K,V]
  })

  def fromMap[S,K,V](m: Map[K,V]): ST[S, STMap[S,K,V]] = ST(new STMap[S,K,V] {
    val table = (HashMap.newBuilder[K,V] ++= m).result
  })
}
```

Answers to exercises for chapter 15

Exercise 15.01

```
def take[I](n: Int): Process[I,I] =
  if (n <= 0) Halt()
  else await(i => emit(i, take[I](n-1)))

def drop[I](n: Int): Process[I,I] =
  if (n <= 0) id
  else await(i => drop[I](n-1))

def takeWhile[I](f: I => Boolean): Process[I,I] =
  await(i =>
    if (f(i)) emit(i, takeWhile(f))
    else      Halt())

def dropWhile[I](f: I => Boolean): Process[I,I] =
  await(i =>
    if (f(i)) dropWhile(f)
    else      emit(i,id))
```

Exercise 15.02

```
/*
 * Exercise 2: Implement `count`.
 *
 * Here's one implementation, with three stages - we map all inputs
 * to 1.0, compute a running sum, then finally convert the output
 * back to `Int`. The three stages will be interleaved - as soon
 * as the first element is examined, it will be converted to 1.0,
 * then added to the running total, and then this running total
 * will be converted back to `Int`, then the `Process` will examine
 * the next element, and so on.
 */
def count[I]: Process[I,Int] =
  lift((i: I) => 1.0) |> sum |> lift(_.toInt)


/* For comparison, here is an explicit recursive implementation. */
def count2[I]: Process[I,Int] = {
  def go(n: Int): Process[I,Int] =
    await((i: I) => emit(n+1, go(n+1)))
  go(0)
}
```

Exercise 15.03

```
/*
 * Exercise 3: Implement `mean`.
 *
 * This is an explicit recursive definition. We'll factor out a
 * generic combinator shortly.
 */
def mean: Process[Double,Double] = {
  def go(sum: Double, count: Double): Process[Double,Double] =
    await((d: Double) => emit((sum+d) / (count+1), go(sum+d,count+1)))
  go(0.0, 0.0)
}
```

Exercise 15.04

```
def sum2: Process[Double,Double] =
  loop(0.0)((d:Double, acc) => (acc+d,acc+d))

def count3[I]: Process[I,Int] =
  loop(0)((_:I,n) => (n+1,n+1))
```

Exercise 15.05

```
/*
 * Exercise 5: Implement `|>`. Let the types guide your implementation.
 */
def |>[O2](p2: Process[O,O2]): Process[I,O2] = {
  p2 match {
    case Halt() => Halt()
    case Emit(h,t) => Emit(h, this |> t)
    case Await(f) => this match {
      case Emit(h,t) => t |> f(Some(h))
      case Halt() => Halt() |> f(None)
      case Await(g) => Await((i: Option[I]) => g(i) |> p2)
    }
  }
}
```

Exercise 15.06

```
// this uses the `zip` function defined in exercise 7
def zipWithIndex: Process[I,(O,Int)] =
  this zip (count map (_ - 1))
```

Exercise 15.07

```
/*
 * Exercise 7: Can you think of a generic combinator that would
 * allow for the definition of `mean` in terms of `sum` and
 * `count`?
 *
 * Yes, it is `zip`, which feeds the same input to two processes.
 * The implementation is a bit tricky, as we have to make sure
 * that input gets fed to both `p1` and `p2`.
 */
def zip[A,B,C](p1: Process[A,B], p2: Process[A,C]): Process[A,(B,C)] =
  (p1, p2) match {
    case (Halt(), _) => Halt()
    case (_, Halt()) => Halt()
```

```
        case (Emit(b, t1), Emit(c, t2)) => Emit((b,c), zip(t1, t2))
        case (Await(recv1), _) =>
          Await((oa: Option[A]) => zip(recv1(oa), feed(oa)(p2)))
        case (_, Await(recv2)) =>
          Await((oa: Option[A]) => zip(feed(oa)(p1), recv2(oa)))
    }

  def feed[A,B](oa: Option[A])(p: Process[A,B]): Process[A,B] =
    p match {
      case Halt() => p
      case Emit(h,t) => Emit(h, feed(oa)(t))
      case Await(recv) => recv(oa)
    }
```

Exercise 15.08

```
/*
 * Exercise 8: Implement `exists`
 *
 * We choose to emit all intermediate values, and not halt.
 * See `existsResult` below for a trimmed version.
 */
def exists[I](f: I => Boolean): Process[I,Boolean] =
  lift(f) |> any

/* Emits whether a `true` input has ever been received. */
def any: Process[Boolean,Boolean] =
  loop(false)((b:Boolean,s) => (s || b, s || b))

/* A trimmed `exists`, containing just the final result. */
def existsResult[I](f: I => Boolean) =
  exists(f) |> takeThrough(!_) |> dropWhile(!_) |> echo.orElse(emit(false))

/*
 * Like `takeWhile`, but includes the first element that tests
 * false.
 */
def takeThrough[I](f: I => Boolean): Process[I,I] =
  takeWhile(f) ++ echo

/* Awaits then emits a single value, then halts. */
def echo[I]: Process[I,I] = await(i => emit(i))
```

Exercise 15.09

This process defines the here is core logic, a transducer that converts input lines (assumed to be temperatures in degrees fahrenheit) to output lines (temperatures in degress celsius). Left as an exercise to supply another wrapper like `processFile` to actually do the IO and drive the process.

```
def convertFahrenheit: Process[String,String] =
  filter((line: String) => !line.startsWith("#")) |>
  filter(line => line.trim.nonEmpty) |>
  lift(line => toCelsius(line.toDouble).toString)

def toCelsius(fahrenheit: Double): Double =
  (5.0 / 9.0) * (fahrenheit - 32.0)
```

Exercise 15.10

```
/*
 * Exercise 10: This function is defined only if given a `MonadCatch[F]`.
 * Unlike the simple `runLog` interpreter defined in the companion object
 * below, this is not tail recursive and responsibility for stack safety
 * is placed on the `Monad` instance.
 */
def runLog(implicit F: MonadCatch[F]): F[IndexedSeq[O]] = {
  def go(cur: Process[F,O], acc: IndexedSeq[O]): F[IndexedSeq[O]] =
    cur match {
      case Emit(h,t) => go(t, acc :+ h)
      case Halt(End) => F.unit(acc)
      case Halt(err) => F.fail(err)
      case Await(req,recv) => F.flatMap (F.attempt(req)) {
        e => go(Try(recv(e)), acc)
      }
    }
  go(this, IndexedSeq())
}
```

Exercise 15.11

```
/*
 * Create a `Process[IO,O]` from the lines of a file, using
 * the `resource` combinator above to ensure the file is closed
 * when processing the stream of lines is finished.
 */
def lines(filename: String): Process[IO,String] =
  resource
    { IO(io.Source.fromFile(filename)) }
    { src =>
        lazy val iter = src.getLines // a stateful iterator
        def step = if (iter.hasNext) Some(iter.next) else None
        lazy val lines: Process[IO,String] = eval(IO(step)).flatMap {
          case None => Halt(End)
          case Some(line) => Emit(line, lines)
        }
        lines
    }
    { src => eval_ { IO(src.close) } }

/* Exercise 11: Implement `eval`, `eval_`, and use these to implement `lines`. */
def eval[F[_],A](a: F[A]): Process[F,A] =
  await[F,A,A](a) {
    case Left(err) => Halt(err)
    case Right(a) => Emit(a, Halt(End))
  }

/* Evaluate the action purely for its effects. */
def eval_[F[_],A,B](a: F[A]): Process[F,B] =
  eval[F,A](a).drain[B]
```

Exercise 15.12

Notice this is the standard monadic `join` combinator!

```
def join[F[_],A](p: Process[F,Process[F,A]]): Process[F,A] =
  p.flatMap(pa => pa)
```

A brief introduction to Haskell, and why it matters

Haskell[215] is in some ways a nicer language for functional programming than Scala, and if you are serious about learning more FP, we recommend learning it. We recommend this even if you continue to program predominantly in Scala. Why? Many of the key ideas and structures covered in this book (for instance, most of parts 3 and 4) originated with research or work using Haskell. Throughout the chapter notes, we have provided links to further reading–many of those references use Haskell, and knowing Haskell at least well enough to 'read' it will let you tap into the enormous well of ideas about FP that exist in the Haskell community. Our goal here is not to make you a Haskell expert, but to give enough of an introduction to the language that you can learn from the various resources (papers, blog posts, and code) about FP that use Haskell.

About Haskell

Haskell is a purely functional language. Unlike Scala, there is no escape hatch–if you want to write imperative code in Haskell, you are forced to use the techniques discussed in part 4–the IO and ST monads, and/or a higher-level library built atop these data types, like the streaming library we discussed in chapter 15. (Technically, Haskell does include some functions, like unsafePerformIO, that allow you to subvert its purity. But these functions are used extremely rarely, as they don't mix well with Haskell's laziness.) This lack of escape hatch has been one reason why many discoveries of how to write functional programs have come from the Haskell community–in Haskell, the question, "how do I express this program using pure functions?" is not merely an intellectual exercise, it is a prerequisite to getting anything done!

Notably, Haskell is also *lazy by default*. As we discussed in chapter 5, Scala (and most other languages) by default evaluates function arguments *before* calling the function. In Haskell, arguments are by default passed unevaluated and data constructors are also lazy. This is a very different model of computation than a strict language, and reasoning about performance in Haskell is different than in a strict language. There are benefits to the Haskell model (we discussed some of these benefits in chapter 5), though if you do start Haskell programming, *take the time to fully understand Haskell's evaluation model and incorporate it into your thinking.*

Note: To be a bit more precise, the Haskell standard does not technically dictate that all functions be call-by-need (lazy) and the compiler/runtime is free to do more strict evaluation so long as this does not affect program behavior. As a general rule, though, call-by-need evaluation provides a reasonable mental model for how Haskell programs are executed.

---

[215]http://www.haskell.org/haskellwiki/Haskell

We won't talk too much more about Haskell's laziness in this appendix, but follow some of the links at the end for more information.

Haskell syntax

Let's start by looking at a simple "Hello world!" program, which we might place in a file, Main.hs:

```
module Main where    -- A comment, starting with `--`

-- Equivalent to `def main: IO[Unit] = ...`
main :: IO ()
main = putStr "Hello world!!"
```

We can compile this using the Glasgow Haskell Compiler[216] (GHC), which comes bundled with the Haskell Platform[217].

```
> ghc --make Main
[1 of 1] Compiling Main             ( Main.hs, Main.o )
Linking Main ...
> ./Main
Hello world!!
```

Module declarations start with the keyword module, then are followed by a module name (here Main, but Foo.Bar.Baz and Data.List are also valid module names), then the keyword where. Like Java, module names must follow directory structure, so Foo.Bar must live in a file called Bar.hs inside the Foo/ directory.

The entry point of a Haskell program is the main function. In Haskell, type signatures *precede* the declaration of the value. So main :: IO () is a type signature, preceding the definition of main = putStr "Hello world!!" on the subsequent line. We pronounce the :: symbol as 'has type'.

Since Haskell is pure, it uses an IO type to represent computations that may interact with the outside world. Unlike Scala, IO is built into the language–you do not need to write your own IO type like we did in chapter 13. And there are a couple other differences in how we write type signatures–the Unit type from Scala is written as () in Haskell. (Like Scala, it has a single value, written ()) And *type application* uses juxtaposition, rather than square brackets. For comparison:

- IO[Unit] (Scala) vs IO () (Haskell)
- Map[String,Double] vs Map String Double
- Map[String,Map[K,V]] vs Map String (Map k v): In Haskell, type variables must begin with a lowercase letter. Names starting with uppercase are reserved for concrete types and data constructor names.

---

[216]http://www.haskell.org/ghc/
[217]http://www.haskell.org/platform/

Modules with explicit export lists

All values and types declared inside a Haskell module are public by default. If you wish to make some of these private, you can declare the module with an explicit *export list*, and simply avoid mentioning any private functions you don't want others to use. For example:

```
module TopSecret (f1, f2) where

f1 :: Int
f1 = f2 + magicValue

f2 = 97
magicValue = 42
```

Since `magicValue` is not exported, it will not be visible to users of this module. See the Haskell wikibook[a] for more information about importing and exporting.

---

[a]http://en.wikibooks.org/wiki/Haskell/Modules#Exporting

Type application is left-associative, so `Foo x y z` is the same as `((Foo x) y) z`. Unlike Scala, type constructors in Haskell are *curried* by default. We do not need to do anything special to partially apply a type constructor, we just leave off some of the arguments (recall the type-lambda trick we introduced in chapter 11 when giving the `Monad` instance for `State`.) We'll see how this comes in handy later, when giving the `Monad` instance for `State`.

Let's look at a couple function definitions:

```
factorial :: Int -> Int
factorial 0 = 1
factorial n = n * factorial (n-1)

factorial' :: Int -> Int
factorial' n = go n 1
  where go 0 acc = acc
        go n acc = go (n-1) (n * acc)

factorial'' :: Int -> Int
factorial'' n =
  let go 0 acc = acc
      go n acc = go (n-1) (n * acc)
  in go n 1
```

A few things about this code:

- Function types are written using -> instead of => as in Scala.
- Identifier names in Haskell can contain the ' symbol (as well as _, letters, and numbers, though data types must start with a capital letter and other identifiers cannot start with a number or ').
- The syntax for *function application* is simple juxtaposition, with arguments separated by spaces, as in go n 1 (vs go(n, 1) in Scala). Function application is left-associative and binds tighter than any other operation, so f x y+1 would actually be parsed as (f x y) + 1, and we can use parentheses to obtain a desired grouping.
- We are also making use of a local function to write our loop in both factorial' and factorial'', much like we'd do in Scala, though unlike Scala, *all tail calls are optimized*. Syntactically, we can place local definition(s) *after* the expression that references it, using a where-clause (used in factorial') or we can place the local definitions *before* the expression referencing it, using a let expression (used in factorial'').
- These examples demonstrate some simple pattern matching in Haskell, matching on the numeric literal 0. We can write a function's name several times, supplying a pattern for each argument. Patterns are matched top to bottom, as in Scala. We'll talk more about Haskell's pattern matching in the next section.

Note: Haskell determines where blocks begin and end based on indentation. Certain keywords (like let and where) introduce a *layout block*. Read all about the details here[218].

Lastly, we note that unlike Scala, Haskell does not have a distinction between val, def, lazy val, and var. All declarations use the same syntax, a symbol name, followed by any arguments or patterns, followed by an = sign, followed by the body of the definition.

Data types and higher order functions

Unlike Scala, algebraic data types in Haskell are not represented using subtypes. Instead, we declare an ADT just by listing its data constructors using the following syntax:

```
data List a = Nil | Cons a (List a)

data Option a -- alternate style
  = None
  | Some a
```

An ADT is introduced with the keyword data, followed by the name of the type, followed by a list of type parameter names separated by spaces, followed by an =, then a list of data constructors separated by |. Each data constructor must start with an uppercase letter (exception: constructors starting with : are allowed, and are useful for infix 'operator' data constructors), and as with function

---

[218]http://en.wikibooks.org/wiki/Haskell/Indentation

application we just separate the arguments of the data constructor by spaces, using parentheses for grouping. Note that data constructor arguments are unnamed, we give only their types. There is a limited form of named accessors in Haskell; see the sidebar below.

Rather than having `Nil` 'extend' `List[Nothing]`, Haskell has proper *universally quantified types*. The type of the value `Nil` is `forall a . List a`, which means that we can treat `Nil` as a `List Int`, a `List String`, and so on, for any choice of `a`.

Note: Haskell also includes a feature called generalized algebraic data types (GADTs), which have a slightly different syntax. GADTs are quite powerful and come up a lot when designing embedded domain specific languages. See the Haskell Wikibook[219] for more information.

As mentioned above, data constructors in Haskell are lazy by default. We could use the `List` data type above to construct an infinite sequence, much like we did for `Stream` in chapter 5.

Pattern matching mirrors the syntax of the data constructors as in `headOption`, which returns the first element of a `List a`, if one exists.

```
headOption :: List a -> Option a
headOption Nil = None
headOption (Cons h t) = Some h
```

Pattern matching forces evaluation of the expression being matched (here, the argument to `headOption`), though the expression is only forced to a depth needed to resolve which branch to take. Thus, `headOption` works fine for an infinite list.

Haskell record syntax

If you want to name the arguments to a data constructor, you can just write functions, for instance (note these are partial functions which generate a pattern match error at runtime if given `Nil`):

```
head (Cons h _) = h
tail (Cons _ t) = t
```

Haskell provides some syntax sugar which generates these functions for you:

```
data List a = Nil | Cons { head :: a, tail :: List a }
```

This is the same `List` type but the `{ head :: a, tail :: List a }` instructs the compiler to generate the `head` and `tail` accessors. Because this simple scheme puts accessors into the module namespace,

---

[219]http://en.wikibooks.org/wiki/Haskell/GADT

you cannot have two data constructors in the same module with a same-named argument. There are various proposals to improve on this.

Note: Haskell does not support ad hoc name overloading like Scala.

Note that the Haskell standard library contains an implementation of `Option`, although the type is called `Maybe`, and its constructors are called `Nothing` and `Just` instead of `None` and `Some`:

```
data Maybe a = Nothing | Just a
```

There is also a data type, `Either` in Haskell, with the same constructors as Scala:

```
data Either a b = Left a | Right b
```

List syntax and higher order functions

Lists in Haskell come built in and have some special syntax. We write the type `List Int` as `[Int]`, we write `Nil` as `[]`, and `Cons h t` as `h:t`. The `:` operator is right-associative, so `1:2:[]` is equal to `1:(2:[])`. And we can write list literals using the syntax `[1,2,3,4]`, `["a","b"]`.

Let's look at a couple familiar higher-order list functions, which will also give us an excuse to discuss some more bits of Haskell syntax:

```
foldRight :: (a -> b -> b) -> b -> [a] -> b
foldRight f z xs = case xs of
  [] -> z
  h:t -> f h (foldRight f z t)

-- signature not needed (see note below)
takeWhile f xs =
  foldRight (\h t -> if f h then h : t else []) [] xs

takeWhile' f =
  foldRight (\h t -> if f h then h : t else []) []
```

Note: In the Haskell standard library, `foldRight` is called `foldr` and `foldLeft` is called `foldl`.

Note: Haskell is fully inferred, unlike Scala, so type annotations are generally not needed anywhere, not even for top-level function declarations (though it is considered good style to include them).

This snippet again shows a few new things. Let's start by looking at the type signature. What's with all the `->` symbols? Functions in Haskell are curried by default. Although we can write `(Int,Int) -> Int`, for the type of a function that expects a pair of integers and returns an `Int`, we almost always work with curried functions in Haskell and the language has special support for interpreting curried function application efficiently. The `->` operator is right-associative, so the type `(a -> b -> b) -> b -> List a -> b` can be read the same way you'd read the Scala signature:

```
def foldRight[A,B](f: (A,B) => B, z: B, xs: List[A]): B
```

Function literal syntax is a bit different in Haskell as well. In Scala, we'd write `(h,t) => ...`, in Haskell, we write `\h t -> ....` The parameters to a lambda function mirrors the syntax for function application, with parameters separated by spaces. Following the parameter list is the `->`, then the body of the lambda. In this case, the function literal we are passing to `foldRight` uses an `if` expression, which uses the syntax `if <expr> then <expr> else <expr>`.

Moving on, we see an alternate syntax for pattern matching the `case ... of` syntax. This is analogous to Scala's `match` expression, and grammatically it can be used anywhere an expression is expected–it's not tied to a symbol delaration like we saw earlier for `factorial`.

Lastly, the definition of `takeWhile'` shows a very common idiom in Haskell. Because functions are curried by default, we get a very lightweight syntax for left-to-right partial application–we simply leave off some of the arguments! In the case of `takeWhile'`, we are leaving off one of its parameters (the list parameter), since all we are doing with it is passing it along to the `foldRight` function. This is called *eta reduction*. More generally, the following three definitions are all equivalent:

```
f x y = g x y
f x = g x -- eta reduction
f = g -- another eta reduction
```

The Haskell Wiki[220] has a nice further explanation.

Generally, function parameters are ordered to maximize the usefulness of left-to-right partial application, which is usually the *opposite* order of typical OO.

Note: In Haskell, you'll often see expressions like `sum (filter isEven (map f xs))` written as: `sum . filter isEven . map f $ xs`. What's going on here? Well, `f . g` is equivalent to `f.compose(g)` in Scala (recall that `f.compose(g)(x) == f(g(x))`). And `f $ x` is equivalent to `f x`, but the `$` has very low precedence and is just used to avoid having to introduce a level of parentheses. This reads "backwards" from the typical OO chain of function calls, where we'd write `xs.map(f).filter(isEven).sum`.

Type classes, monads, and do notation

`Monad`, `Applicative`, `Functor`, and all the other structures we discussed in part 3 exist in Haskell's standard library. The way they are encoded and used works differently than in Scala. Let's start by looking at what is called the *class* definition for `Functor`:

---

[220]http://www.haskell.org/haskellwiki/Eta_conversion

```haskell
class Functor f where
  fmap :: (a -> b) -> (f a -> f b)
```

This is equivalent to the following *interface* definition in Scala:

```scala
trait Functor[F[_]] {
  def fmap[A,B](f: A => B): F[A] => F[B]
}
```

Functor is called a *type class* (or 'typeclass') in Haskell. The name comes from the the the fact that it defines a *class* of types, not in the OO sense of the term 'class', but in the more general, mathematical sense of a collection of objects whose members can be described in some formal way..

Let's now look at how we declare an instance of Functor:

```haskell
instance Functor Maybe where
  fmap f Nothing = Nothing
  fmap f (Just x) = Just (f x)
```

Whereas in Scala, we'd write:

```scala
val OptionFunctor = new Functor[Option] {
  def fmap[A,B](f: A => B): Option[A] => Option[B] =
    oa => oa match {
      case None => None
      case Some(a) => Some(f(a))
    }
}
```

Notice that in Haskell, we aren't naming the instance at all. We simply state "here is the Functor instance for the type constructor Maybe". We'll see why this is in a minute.

The way we write code which is polymorphic in the choice of Functor works differently in Haskell. In Scala, we might accept the Functor instance as an ordinary function parameter, possibly implicit. (We might also just place the definition within the Functor trait.)

```scala
def strength[F[_],A,B](
    a: A, fb: F[B])(implicit F: Functor[F]): F[(A,B)] =
  F.fmap((b: B) => (a,b))(fb)
```

In Haskell, instances are not first-class values as they are in Scala. Instead, we accept Functor as a *constraint*:

```
strength :: Functor f => a -> f b -> f (a, b)
strength a fb = fmap (\b -> (a,b)) fb
-- Or, eta reduced:
-- strength a = fmap (\b -> (a,b))
```

Notice the call to `fmap` in the implementation doesn't say which `Functor` instance it is referring to! Instances are unnamed and the correct instance will be chosen based on type–for instance, when calling `strength 1 ["a", "b", "c"]`, the `Functor` for list will be supplied automatically. Although Haskell frees the programmer from having to explicitly pass instances around in the program, because instances are not first-class values and are selected based on *type*, we are limited to supplying at most one instance for a given type. For instance, we can imagine multiple `Monoid` instances on `Int`, one for addition, and one for multiplication. If `Monoid` is formulated as a `class`, we can't give both instances, as they overlap:

```
class Monoid a where
  mempty :: a
  mappend :: a -> a -> a

instance Monoid Int where
  mempty = 0
  mappend = (+) -- Syntax for referencing an infix operator

-- Not legal! Overlapping instance
instance Monoid Int where
  mempty = 1
  mappend = (*)
```

Note: No one particularly likes the names `mempty` and `mappend`, as they sound a little too specific to lists, but these are the names used in the Haskell standard library definition of `Monoid`.

If both these instances were defined, we would have no way of distinguishing which one was intended at the call site of a function like `foldMap`:

```
foldMap :: Monoid m => (a -> m) -> [a] -> m -- only takes two arguments, no way to specify\
 the instance!
foldMap f = foldr mappend mempty . map f
```

Note: Haskell's restriction on overlapping instances does come with another benefit. If we have two `Map k v` values (Haskell's ordered map implementation), it is safe to assume that both maps were ordered using the same `Ord k` instance (`Ord` is Haskell's typeclass for specifying ordering). This is not in general a safe assumption to make in Scala, as the maps may have been built by two different pieces of code, each of which locally used a different instance of `Ordering` (the Scala trait for specifying ordering).

In situations where we might otherwise define multiple overlapping instances, we can do one of two things. We can switch to using ordinary values to represent the class. For Monoid, we can create a type with a single data constructor, containing the identity and the operation:

Note: By convention, data types with a single constructor usually give the constructor the same name as the type.

```
data Monoid a = Monoid a (a -> a -> a)
```

Or we can provide a wrapper type for Int, simply so Haskell's type system can use this to select the appropriate Monoid:

```
newtype Sum = Sum Int
newtype Product = Product Int

instance Monoid Sum where
  mempty = Sum 0
  mappend (Sum a) (Sum b) = Sum (a + b)

instance Monoid Product where
  mempty = Product 1
  mappend (Product a) (Product b) = Product (a * b)
```

Note that newtype Sum = Sum Int behaves just like data Sum = Sum Int, but its runtime representation is the same as whatever is inside the newtype, in this case Int.

Let's look at the class definition for Monad, and the Monad instance for Maybe and State. This introduces a few new things:

```
class Monad f where
  return :: a -> f a
  (>>=) :: f a -> (a -> f b) -> f b

instance Monad Maybe where
  return = Just

  Nothing >>= _ = Nothing
  Just x >>= f = f x

data State s a = State { runState :: s -> (a, s) }

instance Monad (State s) where
  return a = State $ \s -> (a, s)
  a >>= f = State $ \s0 -> case runState a s0 of
    (ar, s1) -> runState (f ar) s1
```

In Haskell, `unit` and `flatMap` are named `return` and `>>=` (pronounced 'bind'). Notice that we didn't need to construct a type lambda like we did in chapter 11, we just partially applied the `State` type constructor by leaving off its second parameter.

Haskell also includes an analogue of for-comprehension syntax, called `do`-notation. Here's an example:

```
main :: IO ()
main = do
  putStr "Echo-inator v2.0"
  s <- readLine
  putStr s
```

This is equivalent to:

```
main =
  putStr "Echo-inator v2.0" >>= \_ -> -- As in Scala, we use '_' for an ignored function p\
arameter
  readLine >>= \s ->
  putStr s
```

Unlike Scala's `for` comprehensions, we aren't required to end with a `yield`, and we don't have to extract a value from each monadic expression in the `do` block. Here's the equivalent Scala:

```
def main = for {
  _ <- putStr("Echo-inator v2.0")
  s <- readLine
  _ <- putStr(s)
} yield ()
```

Conclusion

This appendix has only scratched the surface of Haskell, but should provide you with a foundation for reading papers, blog posts, and other resources that use Haskell. We recommend the Haskell Wikibook[221] as a good reference for learning more of the details of Haskell's syntax.

---

[221]http://en.wikibooks.org/wiki/Haskell

Made in the USA
San Bernardino, CA
20 June 2015